PASSING ON THE TORCH
AND OTHER SERMONS

Passing On the Torch
And Other Sermons

BY
A. T. ROBERTSON, D.D., LL.D., LITT.D.,
*Professor of New Testament Interpretation, in the
Southern Baptist Theological Seminary,
Louisville, Ky.*

" We preach Christ Jesus as Lord "
2 COR. 4:5

NEW YORK
Fleming H. Revell Company
LONDON   AND   EDINBURGH

New York: 158 Fifth Avenue
London: 21 Paternoster Square

TO
MY SON
ARCHIBALD THOMAS ROBERTSON, JR.

PREFACE

THESE sermons have been preached at different times during the past fifty years, some of them many times, to audiences in country churches, in city churches of various denominations, in colleges and theological seminaries, before Young Men's Christian Associations, Young Women's Christian Associations, Baptist Young People's Union assemblies, Bible conferences, summer assemblies and denominational conventions, in revivals, to city rescue missions, at commencements, to groups of ministers. Chiefly, they are exegetical with a few on Bible characters. Most of my sermons on New Testament persons appear in *Types of Preachers in the New Testament* and in *Some Minor Characters in the New Testament*. All of my life (since 1888) has been devoted to teaching in the theological seminary along with ten years as pastor of country churches in connection with my teaching. But I have always considered myself as primarily a preacher of Christ, though mainly through my students. And yet I must have preached several thousand times myself. These sermons fairly represent my message as a minister of Jesus Christ. May the Spirit of Christ use them for his glory in spite of their many shortcomings.

A. T. R.

Southern Baptist Theological Seminary,
Louisville, Ky.

CONTENTS

I

PASSING ON THE TORCH

"For which reason I am reminding thee to keep blazing the gift of God. . . . Deposit these with reliable men who will be able to teach others also."—2 TIMOTHY 1: 6; 2: 2.

THE title for this sermon is obtained by combining the metaphor of rekindling the spark (*anazōpurein*) in 2 Timothy 1: 6 with the second verse of the second chapter when Paul exhorts Timothy to " deposit " what he had heard from him with reliable men who will be able to teach others also. Timothy with his own fire blazing is to set fire to others who will pass on the torch. Ordinarily we are not to mix metaphors or to combine detached verses of Scripture. One who is skilful at such jugglery with texts can prove any proposition that he wishes. An obvious illustration is this: " Judas went and hanged himself. Go thou and do likewise. And what thou doest, do quickly." But in this instance the result is wholly in accord with the tenor of Second Timothy. Paul is greatly concerned that Timothy shall be able to propagate the gospel message effectively after Paul himself is gone. The metaphor in *anazōpurein* is a graphic one. The present active infinitive expresses linear or continual action. It is a double compound that occurs in the vernacular papyri, but only here in the New Testament. *Pur* is fire, *zōo* is alive, and *ana* means again. The substantive *zōpuron* (a live fire) occurs either for embers (live coals) or for a pair of bellows with which to blow into flame the live coals. So then Paul is here urging Timothy not to let the fire from God in his soul go out, but to fan it into flame. The

11

gift of God is in Timothy, Paul says, but it is up to
Timothy to blow it into a blaze. This simple fact helps
explain why some men of smaller gifts may make a
bigger blaze by blowing harder and longer. In 1 Thessalonians 5: 19 Paul employs the same metaphor of fire
in relation to the Holy Spirit: " Quench not the Spirit."
That is a habit that will put the fire out in any life.
Jesus himself applied the figure of fire to his own
ministry (Luke 12: 49): " I came to cast fire upon the
earth, and what do I wish if it is already kindled " (or
" How I wish that it were already kindled "). Timothy
is to keep his own fire going. We became familiar with
this thought during the World War, when everybody was
singing " Keep the Home Fires Burning."

Five words can be used to bring out Paul's ideas on
this subject in these passages:

1. Inheritance.

Paul is rich in his spiritual inheritance in God whom
he has been serving from his forefathers. He once had
great pride in his Jewish, not to say Pharisaic, ancestry
and environment, and could boast of it on occasion,
though a foolish thing to do, as he knew (2 Cor. 11: 22f.).
Now as a Christian, Paul no longer glories in such things
which are mere refuse in comparison with what Jesus
offers (Phil. 3: 5–11). But Paul still feels gratitude to
God for the pious ancestry that was his and reminds
Timothy too of his debt to his mother Eunice and to
his grandmother Lois. Timothy's tears remind Paul of
his emotional nature and tender regard for the two
women who shaped his training. Timothy's father was
a Greek and so out of this noble line of faith in God
(Acts 16: 1). One may cherish the hope that Timothy
was able to win his own father to faith in Christ. It is
impossible to exaggerate the value of a pious heritage
such as both Paul and Timothy possessed.

Only we must bear in mind that genuine faith such as

Timothy had ("unhypocritical faith") is a personal matter and not a mere matter of inheritance or of heredity, to use the scientific term. That was and is a common fallacy in religion. John the Baptist had to warn the Pharisees and Sadducees who came to his baptism against saying within themselves: "We have Abraham as our father" (Matt. 3: 9; Luke 3: 8), and therefore need no personal change in heart or life. The Jews held that Abraham possessed a superfluity of merit that overflowed to all of his descendants. That is a heresy none too rare to-day with husbands who serve God by proxy. That is, the wife attends church and gives money from the husband while he abstains from outward service to Christ and enjoys his own pleasures and actually has a dim hope of eternal life on the ground of his wife's piety. Such husbands may go to heaven by proxy also. The wife will go to heaven while the husband goes elsewhere.

And yet the child of pious parents does have a better chance of being saved than the children of worldly people and of the slums. It is possible, most assuredly, for men and women of evil ancestry and wicked associations to be converted, radically and completely changed from darkness to light and life. That miracle is one of the continual proofs of the reality and the power of Christianity. We know that Christ is alive to-day because he does lift men and women out of the gutter and set them upon their feet. This is a blessed and a glorious fact and a ground for gratitude. And yet, one who, like Paul and Timothy, comes to Christ out of a Christian home has special reason for gratitude to God for his manifold mercies, for hallowed memories of pious loved ones, for being started when young to walk in the way of life, for the chance of having a long life of Christian growth and service, for the many years of fellowship with Jesus Christ here.

To be sure, not all children from pious homes respond

to their environment. Some react in the other direction and rebel against a mother's prayers and a father's counsel, to show their independence. That is true, but by no means so common as people imagine. There is a popular superstition, sometimes amounting to prejudice, that preachers' sons are worse than those of men of other callings. The stirring examples of such derelicts are allowed to give colour to the whole group. Examination of *Who's Who* has revealed the fact that there are sixteen times as many names of preachers' sons and daughters in that list of notables as there should be in proportion to the number from other callings in life. The child of devout parents has all the advantages in the race for a useful career.

It is a high and holy privilege for a father or mother to lead the child to trust in Christ, one that should be cherished and practised. That is one of life's chief joys as many can testify. Occasionally one finds a father, and even a mother or grandmother, who opposes the child's taking a stand for Christ till he is some fifteen years of age. That is a terrible, and often a fatal, blunder. The child should be allowed and encouraged to give his heart to Christ. Paul reminds Timothy that such an inheritance of faith calls for courage, not cowardice, on his part.

2. *Preparedness.*

Timothy was blessed in his teachers (his mother and his grandmother) who had taught him " the sacred writings." He should never forget that fact nor what he had learned from them. In fact, Timothy himself even as a boy, on occasion had to take his father's place (he being a Greek) and recite the Scriptures himself (acting thus as head of the family). Many a man has stored away in his mind the Scriptures committed to memory when a child. They are still the portions best known and most prized and easiest to use against the tempter, or to console or strengthen oneself in trouble. This process began with Timothy " from a babe," that is, from his childhood. It is one of the tragedies of modern life that so many children are not taught any part of the Bible at home. Some homes, alas, have no Bible. Others have a copy, but neglect it. The Bible is still the best seller of all books, but all too many fail to read it themselves and still more neglect to teach it to their children. Family prayers are no longer common, and our complicated way of living works a hardship on the child. Many public schools are not allowed to have daily readings from the Bible. The Sunday School lessons remain the only help for many, but the lessons are brief and only once a week. The Daily Vacation Bible School supplies a real need in many communities. The preaching service, unfortunately, is not largely attended by the children and even so the preacher does not always open the Scriptures in a helpful manner for them.

But the Scriptures are powerful to-day, as of old, and able to make children and men wise unto salvation through faith in Christ Jesus. It is not bibliolatry that Paul here commands, but the use of the Scriptures to turn one to faith in Christ Jesus. He alone is the Saviour from sin. There is no magic or charm in the Scriptures like an amulet that some superstitious people wear. The Pharisees took scraps of the Old Testament and put them in a box and wore them as " phylacteries " (guards to ward off evil) on the arm or the forehead. The Word of God is a lamp to the feet only when it has illumined the heart and life. " All Scripture is God-breathed and useful for teaching, for reproof, for setting one straight, for training in righteousness." Each item here can be verified in the life of each of us, if he will only give it a chance.

Paul gives the purpose in this use of the Scriptures as a preparation for service, " that the man of God may be fully equipped " (*artios*, an old and common adjective from *arō* to fit, to equip). No one is " fitted " for service without adequate knowledge of the Scriptures. Inefficiency among servants of Christ, preachers included, is largely due to ignorance of the Scriptures. The man who has this equipment is " completely furnished unto every good work." As a boy in Statesville, North Carolina, about 1876, I used to see the horses step promptly to the fire engine when the clock struck twelve, and almost instantly dash off with the engine, so soon as the harness was clamped upon them. They were trained for service. If only church members were trained in the Scriptures, they would as readily respond to every call for service at church or elsewhere, in attendance, in offerings, in soul-winning. There is a mighty army of nominal Christians in the world, but the most of them cannot be counted on for actual response to any call for action. They are not trained in the Scriptures. They feel no sense of responsibility for the work and on-going of the kingdom of God or even of the local church to which they belong. They do not give themselves the proper environment, to use another scientific term, for proper functioning. They wither and dry up and drop away for lack of nourishment. They are not fed on the word of life, but fill their minds and hearts wholly on the movies, the sex magazines and novels, the current whirl in the daily papers. They are not prepared for service and render none. They are non-entities in the work of Christ.

3. *Power.*

The translation " be strengthened " is much weaker than the Greek original *endunamou* (present passive imperative of *endunamoō*, a causative verb to empower, to put power or strength into). Paul employs it three times in the active in a vivid personal sense of Christ as the one who empowers him. So in Philippians 4: 13:

" I have strength for all things in the one who keeps on empowering me " (*en tōi endunamounti me*). Christ is the dynamo of energy for Paul and he has strength or power for all things so long as he is in contact with Christ. This simple fact is the secret of the tremendous dynamic energy in Paul's ministry. In 1 Timothy 1: 12 Paul says: " I am grateful to Christ Jesus our Lord who did empower me " (*tōi endunamōsanti me*), when Jesus seized him on the way to Damascus and turned his life clean round (Phil. 3: 12). Once more in his last Epistle (2 Tim. 4: 17) Paul says: " The Lord stood by me " (*moi parestē*) and empowered me " (*kai enedunamōsen me*). This happened at the last trial in Rome when all had deserted him. Paul by experience knew what it was for the Lord Jesus to stand by his side in the hour of peril. He exhorts Timothy therefore " to keep in touch with the power in the grace in Christ Jesus." Christ for Timothy, as for Paul, is the only source of power. This is the lesson that every preacher has to learn. We read sometimes of Jesus that the power of God was with him to heal and at others that Jesus felt power gone forth from him (Mark 5: 30). Certainly no preacher has the power of God when he is out of touch with Christ. The old preachers used to talk about having liberty in preaching. The Spirit of God was with them on such occasions. The nine disciples who had failed to cast the demon out of the epileptic boy, afterwards asked Jesus privately: " Why could not we cast it out? " (Matt. 17: 19). Two answers are given by Jesus: one the lack of faith (Matt. 17: 20), the other lack of prayer (Mark 9: 29). Both are true. These very apostles on the tour of Galilee when they were sent out by twos did cast out demons; but now, at the foot of the Mount of Transfiguration, they neglected to pray and thus get in touch with God. A prayerless preacher is always a powerless preacher. Many a preacher knows what it is to fail with the very

sermon that once was greatly blessed. He neglected to
get in touch with God by prayer. He was not anointed
with the Holy Spirit.

Electricity in modern life is a superb illustration of
what Paul is here urging upon Timothy. The power in
the electric street cars is not in the track, the car, the
motorman, the conductor, the copper wire, though all
these are necessary. The electricity is carried by the
wire, but the wire is dead without it. With it there is
a live wire and the car moves. Without the electric
current the car stops. Fine churches, organs, choirs,
pulpits, preachers, are all excellent, but without the
power of the Holy Spirit they are all sounding brass and
tinkling cymbals. Once, when I was a student at Wake
Forest College, the professor of electricity asked me to
step upon a small table with four glass rollers so that
it was insulated. Then he turned electricity on me till
my hair stood on end and my clothing would pop and
snap with sparks of electricity. The class were asked
to come around and poke their fingers within a few
inches of me but without touching me. When they did
so, sparks flashed from me to their finger-tips. I was
electrified, charged with power. Alas that it should be
so, but sometimes no power goes out from us for there
is no power in us. We are not in tune with the Infinite.
We are not filled with the Holy Spirit.

The scientific word for God is Energy. Paul describes
God as "the one who energizes (*ho energōn*) in you
both the willing and the energizing of his good pleasure"
(Phil. 2: 13). Great scientists like Jeans and Edding-
ton are willing to recognize God as the primal force in
all nature. That is true in every phase of life as men
are at last coming to see. It is preëminently true of the
life of the Christian. Thus alone shall a revival come
when cold and indifferent disciples come back to God in
Christ and get in touch with the Holy Spirit. Then
they can touch other lives with real results. They can

kindle other fires because they themselves have been
rekindled at the altar of God.

4. Deposit.

The word for deposit is an old verb for placing beside
(*para*). It is common for placing food beside one as
when the five thousand were fed (Mark 6: 41; Luke
9: 16) and the four thousand (Mark 8: 6f.) or on the
table beside one (Acts 16: 34). Then the word takes
the turn of depositing a trust with one for security as
with a bank (Luke 12: 48). The papyri have it for
depositing claims to ownership of property or pledges
or earnest of further payments. Then it is common for
commending one to God for protection (Acts 14: 23;
20: 32). In 1 Timothy 1: 18 Paul employs this verb for
laying a charge on Timothy to fulfil the prophecies made
in his youth. Here Timothy is urged by Paul to deposit
the teachings, " what thou didst hear from me in the
presence of many witnesses," " with reliable men," men
who can be counted on to preserve and pass on the
message of eternal life. In 1 Timothy 1: 12 Paul had
used this same adjective (faithful) of himself " because
he counted me faithful putting me into the ministry,
though formerly a blasphemer and a persecutor and in-
jurious." Paul had tried to live up to Christ's hope
concerning him and was still pressing on in pursuit of
that goal (Phil. 3: 12–16).

The idea of " deposit " or " trust " Paul has in a
kindred word, a substantive, *parathēkē*, which means " a
deposit " (or trust). In 1 Timothy 6: 20 Paul pleads
with Timothy: " O Timothy, guard the deposit." He
enforces the exhortation by a warning in a participial
clause, " Turning away from the profane babblings and
oppositions of falsely named knowledge (Gnosticism,
Paul means, common to-day also), which some profess-
ing missed the mark concerning the faith." Then again
in 2 Timothy 1: 12 Paul is fully persuaded that Jesus

whom he has trusted "is able to guard my deposit
against that day." He has no fear that Christ can fail
as the banker in charge of Paul's spiritual interests.
Jesus remains reliable (*pistos*) even if we are unreliable (*ei apistoumen*), "for he is not able to deny
himself" (2 Tim. 2: 13). No bandit, not even Satan
himself, can break the combination of this divine
treasury "hidden with Christ in God" (Col. 3: 3). No
one will be able to lay anything as a charge against
God's elect or to separate them from the love of God
in Christ Jesus (Rom. 8: 33, 35, 39).

Once again Paul returns to the idea in 1 Timothy
6: 20, the deposit that God has placed in Timothy.
"Guard the noble (or beautiful) deposit through the
Holy Spirit who dwells in us" (2 Tim. 1: 14). God has
made an investment in Timothy as in all his children.
It is up to Timothy to make that investment good. We
can all be grateful that God does invest his grace in
such miserable sinners as we are. His lovingkindness
and tender mercy deal with us in hope and confidence.
That is Paul's feeling about himself as first among
sinners in whom as chief Christ has shown what he can
do with a specimen such as Paul was (1 Tim. 1: 15f.).
Paul's idea is that, therefore, no one should be discouraged. God has a rich treasure in his saints in light,
all sinners saved by grace, all monuments of mercy
and love. This is one tremendous reason why it is
good to see a child give his heart to Christ instead of
coming, after a life wasted in sin, and offering the
fragments unto God. In the ruins at Carthage there has
been found a child's metal bank with a coin worth some
six cents. A financier has figured out that at compound
interest this little coin would now be worth something
in the nonillions, or more than a thousand octillions,
nearer infinity than most of us can imagine. Is there
any way to estimate the worth of a long life consecrated
to the service of Christ?

5. Reduplication.

These reliable men " will be able to teach others also," Paul says. So it has always been in the spread of the gospel. One live coal sets fire to another. Andrew brings his brother Simon to Jesus. John brings James. Philip brings Nathanael. Dr. John R. Mott proved a generation ago that by one winning one the whole world could be brought to Christ in one generation. But often a whole life passes by without bringing another soul to the Master. Personal evangelism is the only way by which the gospel can be successfully brought to the hearts of men. We need preaching, more of it and better, but the personal touch of heart to heart, of life on life is what counts most. I heard D. L. Moody say once in a sermon that he knew of more souls won to Christ by his conversation than by his preaching. And Moody was a wonderfully effective evangelist. Isaiah's lips were touched by a live coal from the altar of God and so he had a tongue of flame. Nature is prodigal in her efforts at the reproduction of life. Seeds fall everywhere, carried by the wind and finding congenial soil. Dr. W. H. Houghton of the Calvary Baptist Church in New York City once asked a prayer-meeting audience of three hundred why they had come to his church. Some came because of the radio, some because of newspaper advertisements, but two hundred and fifty of the members came through personal invitations. We should be drummers for Christ. Some men can live in a Christian community and never have a personal word spoken to them about their soul's welfare. Friends will talk about business, pleasure, politics, the weather, anything, everything, except the most important thing of all which is taboo in many social circles and contacts. But if we are to pass on the torch of eternal life, we must keep our own torch blazing. Even if we do not always light that of our neighbours and friends, we can keep it burning as a witness for Christ. John the Baptist was called by Jesus "the bright and shining light" (John 5: 35). We may not be so bright a light as was John, but we are expected to keep even the lower lights burning. We are all lights for Christ to the world (Matt. 5: 14). If men in darkness turn to us for light and find the light gone out, we can give no witness and no help. John McCrae, in "In Flanders Fields," has a word for us:

> "*To you from failing hands we throw*
> *The torch; be yours to hold it high.*"

II

THE GOSPEL OF WORK

"We must work the works of him that sent me while it is day."—JOHN 9: 4.

THERE is a gospel of work. To-day, when depression has for some years hung like a cloud of despair over the world, millions have clamoured for a chance to work for a living, have felt that machines have triumphed over men, whatever there may be in the fad of technocracy. Many are professional hobos and fear work like a nightmare. But work is an old problem and deserves study on the part of every one. Failure to have an occupation explains the ruin of many a young man of wealth. Failure to learn to work starts many a boy on the road to ruin (two hundred thousand in one year).

1. *Jesus felt the Divine Imperative to Work.*

To the Pharisees, who challenged Jesus for healing the lame man on the Sabbath, he replied: " My Father works hitherto and I work " (John 5: 17). God is the great Worker of the universe. He it is who " energizes " us to will and to work (Phil. 2: 13). The claim of Jesus that he was following the example of his own Father angered the Pharisees more than his healing on the Sabbath so that they sought to kill him. But the Master went steadily on with his work and with his claims. No life of a century in length can compare in magnitude of deeds done with the three brief years of the Master's ministry, as he went about doing good, preaching the gospel of the kingdom, teaching the way of life, healing the sick and the suffering. It is small wonder that at

23

the close of a day's journeying he sat wearily on the curbstone of Jacob's well while the disciples went to Sychar for food. We need not be surprised that he fell asleep on a cushion in the stern of the boat, after a day of incessant teaching and explaining his parables, while the boat rocked in a storm and the disciples feared that they were sinking though they had Jesus with them. Jesus was an itinerant preacher, at first popular in Galilee and then so unpopular there that he had not where to lay his head. But he never wavered or ceased to go on. " We must work the works of him that sent me " (John 9: 4). This Divine necessity Jesus frankly accepted. Often he spent whole nights in prayer with the Father when he felt strength gone out of him, or when the people sadly misunderstood him, or when even his chosen band of disciples failed to sympathize with his dearest hopes and purposes. There was in Jesus the supreme urge to work. According to Carlyle that is the mark of genius. In Jesus it is one of the proofs of his deity. He was and is like his Father in the drive to do his Father's will. Jesus felt the force of Kant's " Categorical Imperative " as no one else has.

2. We are Sharers with Jesus in the Works of God.

The correct text in John 9: 4 is: " We must work the works of him that sent me." Jesus takes the disciples in with him as partners in the work of the Father. The same necessity rests upon us also, not in the same degree, but in a degree commensurate with our relation to the Father. We are co-workers with God (1 Cor. 3: 9) in God's field, in God's building. That is our privilege, our honour, our duty, our glory. And yet how complacently, not to say how indifferently, some Christians bear their part in the common work of the kingdom of God in the world. Too many approach church work, kingdom work of any kind, with the desire to get off with as little as possible. They seem to feel that the burden rests on so many that their portion of the responsibility is very small. They are shirkers, or jerkers, not workers. They forget that work is Christlike, that work is Godlike. Some of the manuscripts in 1 Thessalonians 3: 2 speak of Timothy as a co-worker with God as we all should be. In Colossians 4: 11 Paul describes certain brethren in Rome as " co-workers for the kingdom of God." In 3 John 8 John urges his readers to become " co-workers with the truth." Coöperation with God and with God's people is a needed lesson for us all. Some like to see the work of God done, but prefer that some one else do it. When Christ calls to his service he calls to work with him and for him. We are created in Christ Jesus for good works (Eph. 2: 10). That is part of God's elective plan and purpose. He has drafted us for the war with Satan and sin. There are slackers in business, in the home, in church, people who do not like to wear a yoke of any kind that holds them to the family, the task, the church, the state. They dodge taxes and all responsibility when possible.

3. Paul as a Pattern in Work.

It was Paul's boast that, while in Thessalonica, he worked night and day with his own hands so as not to place a burden upon any one of them (1 Thess. 2: 9; 2 Thess. 3: 8). He stopped at the house of Jason (Acts 17: 7), but clearly supported himself by his trade of tent-making as he did later in Corinth and in Ephesus: " Nor did we eat anything freely from any one " (2 Thess. 3: 7). He paid for his meals. Paul claimed the right (2 Thess. 3: 9) to support by the Thessalonians, but he renounced it to remove any charge of covetousness against him (1 Thess. 2: 5). He made the same claim for his work in Corinth, but refused to receive pay for it for the same reason (1 Cor. 9: 3–23). In Corinth in spite of Paul's independence, he was accused of working for money because he sent Titus to raise money for the poor

Christians in Jerusalem (2 Cor. 13: 17f.). He even
" robbed other churches " (2 Cor. 11: 8) from Macedonia
while in Corinth to stop such slander about him. In
Ephesus he desired no man's silver and gold, but with
his own hands wrought for his own needs and for those
of Priscilla and Aquila (Acts 20: 33f.). The modern missionary confronts precisely the same problem that Paul
faced. He must either receive support from elsewhere
or support himself. Paul did both, but would not receive
support from the mission field where he was. In doing
this Paul wrought " in toil and distress." Three times
he connects together these two words (1 Thess. 2: 9; 2
Thess. 3: 8; 2 Cor. 11: 27). If any one thinks that Paul
had an easy time in his work for Christ, let him read
Paul's own list of his toils and sufferings in reply to the
sharp-tongued critics in Corinth (2 Cor. 11: 23-33). It
is enough to make every glib critic of preachers and missionaries ashamed of himself. There are some lazy
preachers as there are some lazy people in the world,
but most people and most preachers are not lazy. There
are some as lazy as the law allows and more so, but they
are not the people who, like Paul, do the world's work
and turn the world upside down. Paul dared demand
that the Thessalonian Christians " imitate " him in his
work and toil (2 Thess. 3: 7). He insists that they knew
already this obligation, " how ye must imitate us." He
had toiled as he did to give himself as a model or " type "
for them in this very matter (2 Thess. 3: 9) that they
might imitate him. Paul recognized frankly that Christians took the preacher as a " type " (Phil. 3: 17), particularly if he did anything questionable or off colour by
which they could justify their own shortcomings. The
church in Thessalonica by its evangelistic activity soon
became a model or type for all believers in Macedonia
(1 Thess. 1: 7). Paul exhorts Timothy to become a
model for all believers in life and preaching (1 Tim.
4:12) and Titus to present himself as a " pattern " in

good works (Tit. 2: 7). Some preachers, forsooth, work
too hard at school and on the field and break down.
They feel that it is better to wear out than to rust out.
That is true, but, as John A. Broadus was fond of saying,
it is not necessary to do either. Broadus was a man of
delicate physique who did a prodigious amount of work
and yet lived to be sixty-eight, about the age of the
apostle Paul. Paul was a man of herculean labours,
whose work in time changed the face of the Roman
Empire and so of the world.

4. *Pious Piddlers Have No Right to Eat.*

Paul had no sympathy with the view, so common to-
day, that the world owes every man a living. The world
owes nothing of the kind, nor does God. Paul's preaching at Thessalonica had been misunderstood on the subject of the second coming of Christ. Paul, like every
preacher who says anything, was continually misunderstood, as was the Lord Jesus himself. In Thessalonica
Paul was accused of saying that Jesus was another king
(Acts 17: 7), the rival of Cæsar, the very charge made
by the Sanhedrin to Pilate against Jesus. That charge
was true of Jesus and of Paul in the spiritual sense of
"king," but the Sanhedrin wanted Pilate to take it in
the political sense and the politarchs in Thessalonica
meant it only in that sense. No doubt Paul in Thessalonica had enlarged upon the kingdom of the Lord Jesus
Christ and had expressed the hope of Christ's early return to earth, as all the early Christians hoped. He had
expressly told them that no one knew when that blessed
hope would be realized: " Now concerning the times and
seasons, brethren, you have no need of my writing to
you, for you yourselves accurately know that the Lord's
day comes as a thief at night " (1 Thess. 5: 1f.). They
knew this " accurately " because Paul had so instructed
them when he was with them. There was no real occasion for their misinterpretation of his words on the sub-

ject. They had misunderstood Paul also about the events when Jesus does come, whether the dead will share in that glorious event. So Paul had already (1 Thess. 4: 13–18) carefully explained that the dead in Christ will be raised before those still alive are changed when all will be caught up to meet Christ in the air and so be forever with the Lord. But the excitement at Thessalonica grew so serious that, in spite of Paul's denial in First Thessalonians, some even claimed that they had a special epistle or message from Paul to the effect that the day of the Lord was right at hand (2 Thess. 2: 2), committing a forgery for the benefit of their theory. Paul flatly denies having ever said so and reminds his readers that his genuine Epistles have his signature in his handwriting (2 Thess. 3: 17). What a treasure one of those autographed manuscripts would be!

But the cranks at Thessalonica showed their particular type of orthodoxy by being too pious to work. These men were perfectly willing to live off of their more diligent neighbours, while they hurried hither and thither informing people precisely when the Lord would appear and getting their ascension robes for exhibition if not for use. Precisely this phenomenon occurred in the states of New Jersey and California (Los Angeles) some years ago when some overwrought people sold their property and bought ascension robes to be ready at a certain hour of a certain day when they had learned (!) that the Lord would appear. Paul gives a vivid picture (2 Thess. 3: 11) of these pious piddlers in Thessalonica, " doing nothing but doing around " (*mēden ergazomenous alla periergazomenous*, a pretty pun, in fact). These pious parasites were merely sponges on the rest of the community and refused to do anything but gad around and misrepresent Paul and his preaching. They were theological deadbeats, fooling around, whittling sticks, telling yarns, cracking jokes, with the philosophy of the hobo. The dole may be necessary in England as we have to have a community chest in our American cities, but the professional beggar meets one at every turn and makes the work of giving real help to the deserving more difficult. The ruin of Rome came when the mob cried for bread and games from the hands of the emperor and quit working. These Thessalonian cranks were pleading the blessed hope of Christ's second coming as an excuse for not working at their daily tasks. They were in too exalted a state of ecstasy to make their own living, to earn their daily bread. Finally Paul reminds them of what he used to tell them when he was with them: "If any one is not willing to work, not even let him eat" (2 Thess. 3: 10). This is blunt, but it can be understood. Paul saw the beginnings of this heresy in creed and conduct while he was in Thessalonica. The evil had grown tremendously since Paul's departure and in spite of his first Epistle to them. Now Paul pointedly commands that the saints in Thessalonica stop feeding these idlers who do nothing but make a disturbance. Paul is the very man who with Barnabas carried to Jerusalem generous gifts from the Greek Christians in Antioch to the poor saints in Jerusalem who had been boycotted by the hostile Jews there in an effort to stop the spread of Christianity in the city. Later Paul will carry a great collection for this group in Jerusalem from the provinces of Asia, Galatia, Macedonia, and Achaia. But the situation in Thessalonica is utterly different. It is due simply to fanatical hysteria and calls for condemnation and firm treatment. The doctrine that Paul here proclaims is not that of modern socialism, communism, or bolshevism. These men had their regular business connections and tasks and gave them up in excitement and persevered in their hallucinations to the injury of all that is good.

5. They Were Walking Disorderly.

Three times in the passage in 2 Thessalonians 3: 6–12 Paul alludes to this result. Those who were " doing nothing but doing around " were " walking disorderly " (*ataktōs*), a military term used of soldiers out of line in march or conduct, especially those disobedient to orders (so in Plutarch). Paul himself while with them " had not acted in disorderly fashion " (verse 7). Paul had given them the right example for soldiers and the proper instruction, " according to the traditions which ye received from us " (verse 6). He had done this while there in person. He repeated it in 1 Thessalonians 4: 10f.: " Now we exhort you, brethren, to abound still more and to be ambitious to be quiet and to do your own affairs and to work with your hands, as we commanded you, that you keep on walking becomingly toward those without and have need of nothing." That should have been plain enough. But he returns to the subject, because these " walking delegates " of religious bolshevism continued their disturbances. They appointed themselves regulators of family life, church life, school life, state life. They were propagandists of evil. " Now such persons we command and exhort in the Lord Jesus Christ that working with quietness they eat their own bread " (2 Thess. 3: 12). They are to earn their own bread and then to eat it and to do it all with becoming quietness and composure. One is not necessarily glorifying God by making a noise, creating excitement, or starting a furor. There are still misguided souls like the " Holy Rollers " who imagine that a nervous frenzy is proof of inspiration and piety. The best work is done in quietness and composure. The still small voice of God is not in the earthquake or the tempest. The noises at the great Pentecost were not the Holy Spirit, but simply the outward proof of the coming of the Dispensation of the Holy Spirit. We are still in that day. What we need to-day is to let the Holy Spirit use us.

Paul has a final word for the stubbornly disobedient one in the church: "If one does not obey our word by the epistle, mark this one, so as not to associate with him, that he may be made ashamed. And yet do not consider him as an enemy, but admonish him as a brother" (2 Thess. 3: 14). What wise words these are to-day for one's attitude toward a contumacious recalcitrant Christian whose views and conduct we cannot approve. A line of cleavage has to come, but let it be so as to win the man back to quiet and balanced service to Jesus Christ if possible. The withdrawal may become necessary (2 Thess. 3: 6). It is necessary, if one continues to be a perverse busybody creating discussions and disturbance. The work of the world and of Christ must go on. The workers are the ones who find joy in life and whose activities go on in heaven (Rev. 14: 13). There our "works" (*erga*) go on, not in the Swedenborgian sense, but in glorified service. We shall rest from our "toils" (*kopōn*), for all weariness will be gone. Meanwhile the watchword of the late Gessner Harrison, of the University of Virginia, may well be ours: "Fear God and work."

III

HUMBLED UNDER GOD'S HAND

"Be humbled therefore under the mighty hand of God that he may exalt you in due season."—1 PETER 5: 6.

PETER probably wrote this epistle from Rome (mystical Babylon, 1 Pet. 5: 13) about A. D. 65 or 66. Nero's persecution of Christians began in A. D. 64 after he had set fire to the city and found it necessary to lay the blame on somebody else than himself. The persecution spread to the eastern provinces where Peter had been preaching (1 Pet. 1: 1). Paul was set free fortunately before the burning of Rome. We do not know why Peter came to Rome at this time, but he draws a practical lesson for the persecuted saints from the fiery trials which they were enduring (1 Pet. 1: 7). John Burroughs, the famous naturalist, had an article a number of years ago in which he said that some people in Virginia still believed in the Providence of God. That is true of millions of other believers outside of Virginia who look to a personal and loving God who rules the universe by his own laws and his own will. We are getting away from the mechanistic conception of the universe that fettered John Burroughs. The greatest modern scientists freely place mind or spirit before and above matter. So then one is not necessarily an ignoramus who cherishes Peter's attitude of humility under God's hand. Peter speaks out of rich and varied experiences. He was not always qualified to speak worthily on the subject of humility, but he is by this time. We are always sure of this about Peter, that his very weaknesses are so much like our own that there is a bond of sympathy between us.

1. Humility and Service.

The " therefore " in verse 6 points back to the preceding paragraph. Peter exhorts humility in view of its necessity for service to others. This Greek word (*tapeinophrosunē*) does not occur in the old Greek writers nor in the Septuagint nor in the papyri (so far as known). It does occur in Josephus and Epictetus in the sense of pusillanimity. Gladstone is quoted (*Life*, iii. p. 466) as saying that " humility as a sovereign grace is the creation of Christianity." The bad sense of the word as an affected and ostentatious humility occurs in Colossians 2: 18, 23, the mock humility like that of the infamous Uriah Heep in *David Copperfield* who was constantly saying " I'se humble," while practising his worst rascalities and duplicities. The gospel of Christ has lifted " low " into " lowly " (Jas. 1: 9f.). Humility is an unconscious grace with the bloom of the rose. In this spirit Peter has a special word.

(a) A Word to Elders.

He employs " elders " here in an official sense like that in Acts 11: 30; 15: 2, etc. as equivalent to " bishops " (Acts 20: 17, 28; Tit. 1: 5, 7), just as our word elder has gone into " alderman." Peter is an apostle (1 Pet. 1: 1), but, like John in 2 and 3 John, he terms himself here " a fellow-elder " on a level with the other pastors or shepherds of the flock of God. He is not posing as a pope or overlord or thinking of himself in that light. But he does claim to be a witness (*martus*, martyr) of the sufferings of Christ and probably with a reminder of the promise of Christ about Peter's death as a martyr in our sense of the word (John 21: 18f.). But all disciples are to be " witnesses," in the original sense (Acts 1: 8), of what they themselves know of Christ's dealings

with them. So Paul glories in that he in his turn is
having his share of the sufferings of Christ (Col. 1: 24).
Peter also claims that he will be a partaker or partner
in the glory of Christ which will be revealed. Here
again he is like Paul: " If indeed we suffer with him,
that we may also be glorified together with him " (Rom.
8: 17). And the glory will far outshine the sufferings
(Rom. 8: 18) and outweigh the tribulations (2 Cor. 4:
17f.).

Peter's exhortation to the elders is to " tend " or shepherd the flock of God, using one of the very words (John
21: 16) employed by Jesus in his charge to him on that
never-to-be-forgotten morning by the Sea of Galilee.
The Gospel of John was not yet written, but these words
are graven on Peter's heart since that morning when
Jesus restored him to fulness of fellowship. Then Peter
was humbled to the earth before the six other brethren.
Now he is himself humble enough to urge it upon other
ministers. Peter's idea of the true shepherd of the flock
of God is like that of Jesus the Good Shepherd in John
10: 1–18 whom Peter here calls the Chief Shepherd
(1 Pet. 5: 4). These elders (shepherds) will exercise the
oversight as bishops (*episkopountes*, so many manuscripts, from *episcopos* bishop) over the flock, not by
compulsion as taskmasters, but with joy and gladness
like that of Jesus over the harvest in Samaria (John 4:
34–36). In particular, they are not to labour " for filthy
lucre " or " for shameful gain " as the rare Greek adverb
means. Likewise Paul warned ministers against being
greedy of filthy lucre (1 Tim. 3: 8; Tit. 1: 7). Already
Satan was using money as a snare with which to catch
preachers. The preacher who preaches for money is sure
to fail both as a preacher and as a money-getter. As a
rule, the preacher who makes or marries money is sure
to get the preacher's sore throat or some other ailment.
The true shepherd responds eagerly to the cry of the
sheep in distress and will leave the ninety and nine in

the fold to go out after the one lost sheep in the mountains. They are not to lord it over the charges allotted to them as small tyrants over a bunch of slaves. In the large cities each church had at first many elders (bishops, shepherds). But here the idea seems rather that each shepherd has his own flock as was doubtless the case from the first in the small and isolated congregations and the churches that met in the houses of various individuals. Each presbyter or elder may have had charge of a particular church house (Bigg.). This lording it over others is condemned by Jesus as heathenish and wholly unbecoming a disciple (Luke 22: 25f.). Arrogance, tyranny, domineering do not fit a minister of Jesus Christ. In a word the preacher is to be a model (type) for the flock. This word of Peter for preachers is the ideal, though Peter himself had not always set a model example in all respects. Like priest, like people. Peter promises the amaranthine or unfading crown of glory to such shepherds when the Chief Shepherd is manifested, as he will be in due time. The amaranth is a flower that rarely withers and quickly revives in water and grows again. That reward will be according to one's real work (1 Cor. 3: 8) and that praise will come from God (1 Cor. 4: 5) and will overtop all the passing flatteries from the lips of men with Paul (1 Thess. 1: 5) and with all of us.

(b) A Word to Young People.

Peter uses " younger " here in contrast to the original meaning of " elder," not the official sense just before. Paul makes a like change in the use of " elder " for age in 1 Timothy 5: 1 and for office in verse 17. It is a natural transition in thought. In both instances reverence is urged for age on the assumption that wisdom belongs to the old. That ought to be true, though it is by no means universal. Japan used to have the Elder Statesmen, a group of men without office who yet exercised dominating influence over the nation's affairs. Certainly it ought to be true that young people find wisdom and piety as well as love in the older members of their family and circle of friends to whom they naturally look for guidance. It is not always easy for the younger to be in subjection to the elder as Peter here urges. In China it is part of their religion to reverence age and to worship one's parents after their death. Sometimes the aged do not deserve respect and forfeit their place of leadership and the young have to step to the front if any forward movement is made. There is a revolt of youth in a good sense as well as in a bad sense. But, as a rule, when the young rebel against the elder people, there is occasion for the older ones to take stock of their own conduct before it is too late. The ideal state is when the father and sons work together in the kingdom of God, each contributing his own special gift for the benefit of all. The aged Apostle of Love has beautifully pictured this response of young and old to the call of Christ for the highest and the best (1 John 2: 12–16).

(c)   A Word to All of Whatever Age or Office.

Peter now succinctly enjoins humility on all individuals of whatever age and upon all classes. He uses a vivid figure for " girding " with humility as if with a towel. Hesychius has *egkomboma* for a blacksmith's apron and the word *kombos* occurs for a knot. Peter's verb occurs nowhere else save in a fragment by Epicharmus. Peter apparently is recalling that graphic incident in his life when Jesus put on a towel and took a basin of water and came to wash his feet (John 13: 4–16), giving them all an " example " of humility which the apostles greatly needed at that moment. Slaves wore a white scarf or apron as a token of their service. Nurses to-day in the hospital wear a uniform as a mark of their professional skill and readiness to serve the sick. It is thus a beautiful picture that Peter here presents. No one is qualified for service to others without true humility, least of all a preacher who puts on an air of self-conscious importance in his visits to the sick in soul and body. This quality of humility, considered a vice by pagans, is absolutely essential if the Christian wishes to do service for Christ who invited all to come to him because he was "meek and lowly in heart" (the very word *tapeinos* employed by Peter). People will not turn to a toploftical conceited physician or preacher who lacks sympathy however gifted he may be in intellect. The sympathetic word and the kindly handshake will lighten the heart and act as medicine to the soul. Besides, God resists the proud, but gives grace to the humble.

2. Humility and Trust.

Humility becomes us all in our relation to God. "Be humbled therefore under the mighty hand of God." It is just because we can find protection under God's hand that we can be content in the midst of untoward circumstances. Paul exhorts us to "glory in tribulations" (Rom. 5: 3), not because of them, but rather because even in the midst of trouble we feel the touch of God's hand and hear the whisper of his love. The Christian is not a cynic like the one who organized a "discontented club" with the motto: "Anywhere but where I am, anything but what I have, and the best is good enough for me." Serenity of temper is possible to the one who trusts God as his Father. Jesus exhorts us not to become anxious about food or clothing (Matt. 6: 31) and to quit it if we have the habit of overanxiety (Matt. 6: 25, 34). Let us get under God's hand.

(a) Because His Hand Is Loving.

"Cast all your anxiety upon him for he does care for you." One of the Psalmists in a pessimistic mood says: "No man cares for my soul." Menander bluntly says: "I have sacrificed to gods that do not care for me."

That was true and it is true of multitudes of modern
pagans who worship the gods of gold and pleasure and
power. But God does care for he is our Father (Luke
21: 18). We can come to him as frankly as our little
children come to us with their wants and their troubles.
We ask our Heavenly Father for forgiveness and for
daily bread. Jesus stands before us all and invites us:
" Come unto me, all ye that toil and are burdened, and I
will refresh you " (Matt. 12: 28). That majestic picture
of God's love looms up above all the turmoil of the
world. God loves us and spared not his own Son for
us.

(b)   Because His Hand Is Mighty.

There is comfort in God's powerful hand. God is able
as well as willing to help us in time of need (Heb. 4:
16). To be sure, Satan as a roaring lion is going his
rounds seeking to devour any one in his path. He is out
to frighten by his roar, for noise is a tremendous and
conclusive argument with many people. One she-wolf
on the prairie can make the welkin ring. But we have
the Lion of the tribe of Judah on our side and he will
prevail over all the wild beasts of hell. What we need,
then, is courage to resist the devil, steadfast in our faith.
Resist the devil and he will flee from you. But in order
to fight the devil successfully we will need to be sober
and alert. " Satan trembles when he sees the weakest
saint upon his knees." There is a *Dies Iræ* coming for
all the enemies of Christ.

> " *Be thou the trembling sinner's stay,*
> *Though heaven and earth shall pass away.*"

The Book of Revelation is a masterful picture of the
age-long conflict of the two lions, Christ and Satan,
for the conquest of the City of Man Soul. Christ will

win in the end. Meanwhile we need to be Greathearts
in faith and courage. Bunyan in *Pilgrim's Progress*
describes Christian on the Hill Difficulty terrified by the
roar of lions. He feared to go on and thought of turning
aside. But on going up he found a lion on each side
chained. They could only roar.

(c) Because Suffering Is the Common Lot of the Broth-
     erhood.

"The same tax of sufferings is paid by your brotherhood in the world." This is the probable meaning of
the rather peculiar idiom here employed. Xenophon
has the same phrase for paying the tax of old age. True
Christians learn how to pay the tax of suffering without
murmuring or complaining (Phil. 2: 14). We have a
saying that misery loves company and there is some
truth in it. It is not that we rejoice that our friends and
neighbours have suffering, but rather that ours is not a
peculiar case. They cannot come around like Job's comforters and try to explain how our peculiar misfortunes
came upon us and not upon them. The disciples soon
learned to rejoice that they were counted worthy to
suffer dishonour for the Name (Acts 5: 41). It is Peter
alone who employs here and in 2: 17 the term "brotherhood" (*adelphotēs*, already in First Maccabees and Dio
Chrysostom) for the whole body of believers. The use
of "brother" for members of the same order or guild
was already common. But the greatest secret order of
all time is the brotherhood in Christ Jesus, bound together by his blood and loving each other (1 Pet. 2: 17),
because we love Jesus supremely. There are three million tombs in the catacombs at Rome of those who were
faithful to Jesus unto death. So we stand in our lot as
good soldiers of Jesus Christ and fight the good fight to
the end, even if, like Paul (Eph. 6: 19f.), we become am-
bassadors in chains. We do not have to court martyr-
dom with mock heroics as some misguided souls have

always done. We have simply to carry on in the spirit of Christ.

3. *Humility and Hope.*

Hope in God is linked with trust in him. We are saved by hope, Paul says (Rom. 8: 24).

(a) We Have God's Promise of Strength.

So we fall back upon God's promise, as Peter does here. "The God of all grace who called you to his eternal glory in Christ shall himself perfect, stablish, strengthen you" (5: 10). That is strong enough to stay any soul, for God has all the grace and glory and strength needed to carry out this promise. God's hand may be unseen to others, but you and I know that it guides our lives. It seems like a mystery for the director of the orchestra to wave his wand over the musicians' heads and draw the varied notes from each that make the harmony for the whole. God plays upon all the chords of the soul in his own wondrous way and for his glory to make each life a harmony in tune with the Infinite. The builder may seem slow in perfecting the building which he has planned, but in the end it will stand complete and satisfying. So we need to put our lives in the hands of the great Architect that he may fashion us according to his own will. Man proposes, but God disposes. The only perfect life is the one that carries out God's plan for that life. That was wholly true of the Son of God. It can only be relatively true of us with our sins and weaknesses, but we should let our lights so shine that men may glorify God when they see something of Christ in us.

(b) In Due Season Comes Exaltation.

"That he may exalt you in due season." That is God's purpose, but it will be in God's time, not in ours. Here is the call for patience. Jesus was fond of saying:

"Every one who exalts himself shall be humbled and the one who humbles himself shall be exalted" (Luke 14: 11). He illustrated the point by a man who at a feast took a high seat and had to be invited to take a lower one in the presence of all. Peter says that true exaltation will come "after ye have suffered a little while." It seems a long while during the suffering but after it is over, there is joy forevermore. Joy comes in the morning after the night of sorrow. It will come in God's own good time. The Scotch have a saying: "When the song's gone out of your life, you can't start another while it is still a ringing in your ears. It is best to have a bit of silence, and out of that maybe a psalm will come by and by." We are not ready for the new song just yet. Henry Austin has said:

> "Out of the presses of pain
> Cometh the soul's best wine.
> The eyes that have shed no rain
> Can shed but little shine."

(c) Brighter Glory Often After Darkest Suffering.

After our suffering in the cloud and storm we may enter into God's eternal glory in Christ. Paul has wondrously put this truth: "For our momentary lightness of affliction is working out for us more and more exceedingly an eternal weight of glory" (2 Cor. 4: 17). The balanced contrast makes the present affliction seem light as a feather, when we look back on it from the standpoint of the eternal glory of God in which we then are. In fact, the glory will actually seem brighter, if possible, because of the dark background of the present life. One day in August, 1890, three of us (J. H. Farmer, L. O. Dawson, and myself) spent the night on Mount Rigi in order to see the sunrise next morning, for it was held to be the grandest sight on earth. We were awakened very early by the Alpine horn and were soon up and out of

the hotel with the other guests on the summit of the
Rigi. It was cold and bleak and we were shivering and
sleepy. We were doomed to disappointment, for soon a
heavy cloud gathered on Mount Pilatus across Lake Lu-
cerne and swiftly swept toward us. The sun rose with
feeble light, flared, flickered and disappeared. We were
compelled to go back to the hotel. My companions returned to bed while I sat by the window and watched
the play of the storm on the mountain peaks as it glow-
ered menacingly above. By and by a faint streak of
light appeared on the snowy peak of Finster-Aarhorn
through a break in the clouds like a taper that crept
down the mountain sides as if the god of the morning
was lighting the candles of day. Soon the Eiger and
the Wetterhorn glimmered and shimmered in golden
glory. The Jungfrau blazed up in majesty to greet the
sun. The sunlight danced from peak to peak along the
whole Bernese Oberland. I roused my companions and
rushed back to the summit of the mountain. I was lost
in the wonder of a sunrise on Mount Rigi, all the more
marvellous because of the black storm that had preceded
it. And, sooth to say, the grandeur of the glory was
greatest right where the blackest storm had been. God
had spread the mantle of his glory over the very mountains that were hid in the storm.

IV

CHRIST'S PLEA FOR THE CHILDREN

"Suffer the little children to come unto me; forbid them not; for of such is the kingdom of God."—MARK 10: 14.

WE owe the modern child's world to Jesus. It has been slow enough in coming at that, but it might never have come but for the new attitude shown by Jesus toward children. Even the apostles rebuked the parents of some children for bringing them to Jesus for him to lay his hands upon their heads, to pray for them, and to bless them. Little attentions like this often make a lasting impression on a child. I can recall to this day the tender touch of a white-haired Episcopal minister's hand upon my head, when only six or seven years old, as I stood on the front steps of my father's home, Cherbury Cottage, in Pittsylvania County, Virginia. All that he said, as his hand rested on my head, was: "God bless you, my boy, and make a preacher of you." That word left its mark on my heart and my life.

In the Græco-Roman world of the first century A. D. infanticide was common and the Roman world was crimson with the blood of infants. The father claimed the right to decide whether the child should be allowed to live or not, horrible as that idea seems to us. In the Oxyrhynchus Papyri (Number 744 B. C. 1) there is a letter from a father to his wife, Hilarion to Alis, in which he says: "If it is a male, let it live; if it is a female, expose it." There it is blunt and brutal. A girl baby was not wanted by that father. That idea is common in China to-day. The Jews did not show this barbarous point of view. The apostles merely objected to the Master being bothered by the children when so many adults were claiming his attention. Some preachers today really do not like to have children in the public worship for fear of some restlessness while they are preaching. Let us see the attitude of Jesus toward children.

1. We See Jesus Loving the Children.

The mothers of the children understood the heart of Jesus better than his own disciples. They somehow felt that Jesus was a preacher who would look kindly upon their little darlings and so they dared to bring them to him, in spite of the big crowd of grown folks, that he might touch them tenderly and pray for them (Matt. 19: 13). They were shocked at the rebuff from the apostles, but Jesus in turn shocked the apostles for their interference and for their lack of love for little children and for their ignorance of his own attitude toward them. Mark (10: 16) observes that Jesus took the little children one after the other in his arms and blessed them, to the joy of the proud mothers and of the happy children. This act of tenderness on the part of Christ did not mean at all that the children were already in the kingdom of God, as some modern theologians hold, but simply that Jesus loved them and rejoiced at the opportunity to bless them and the mothers. It is Mark (9: 36) who previously mentions the fact that Jesus took a little child in his arms, apparently in Peter's house (9: 33) and possibly Peter's own child, when he gave the apostles an object lesson to reprove their jealous ambition as to who was the greatest among them. Possibly in both instances Mark derived this detail from Peter's preaching. Luke (9: 47) notes that Jesus set the little child in Peter's house down by his side right in the midst of the disputing apostles (Matt. 18: 2). Jesus discovered childhood for us all because he loved the child with peculiar tenderness and he loves him now.

Jesus made room for the child in his own heart and so has made room for him in the world. We owe the modern interest in child training to Jesus.

2. Jesus Calling for the Children.

In the scene in Peter's house Jesus " called to him a little child " (Matt. 18: 2). Then again Luke (18: 16) says that Jesus " called " the little children to him when the disciples had sought to push them away. It is perfectly clear that Jesus wanted the little ones to come to him to receive his caresses and his blessing. He did not consider the presence of the children a nuisance or a bother. " Suffer the little children to come unto me." This is a positive plea to all, including the apostles, to let the children come to Christ. In this context the coming was for the affectionate caress and blessing of Jesus, but all the more does it apply to the coming of the child to Christ with the surrender of his heart and life to him. The plea of Jesus here cannot, I think, be rightly used as an argument for infant baptism or infant church membership. But it is a plea for the right of the child to come of his own volition to Christ. Jesus rejoiced to hear the boys crying in the temple " Hosanna to the Son of David " and justified their enthusiasm by saying that God had thus perfected praise out of the mouth of babes and sucklings (Matt. 21: 15f.). It is a glorious thing to see a child give his heart to Christ and serve God with a whole life instead of with just a fragment of a life mostly wasted in sin. There is a particular peril in our own time that with many children the Sunday School may take the place of the church. So many children who go to the Sunday School do not stay to church, never take an active stand for Christ, never join the church, and so finally drop out of the Sunday School and drift back into the world. There is a screw loose here in our modern ecclesiastical machinery when the Sunday School, which was designed to win the young to Christ, has become a substitute for the church of Christ. Most of our church members come from the Sunday School, but many slip by. If the child does not learn the habit of public worship, the man will probably not have it. Thousands of modern Sunday School children do not have the habit of public worship in church and are never won to Christ. Jesus had the habit of worship in the synagogue which he formed as a boy in Nazareth (Luke 4: 16). It is a heart-breaking experience for the preacher to see the children and often the teachers and young people trooping away from Sunday School and not attending church. Jesus wants the children. The problem comes home to parents. Are you winning your own children to Jesus? If not, why not? The problem comes home to the teachers in the Sunday Schools. Are you winning your pupils to Christ? If not, why not?

3. Forbidding Hindrances in the Way of the Children.

"Forbid them not to come unto me." Literally "stop hindering them from coming to me" (Matt. 19: 14). This is precisely what the apostles had been doing in their zeal to relieve the Master from the bother of fond mothers and their children. It was a clear case of zeal without knowledge. Jesus was moved with indignation at this effort to keep the children away from him. Many children, even in pious homes, know what it is to feel that they are in the way, that children are to be seen and not heard, and not always to be seen. The habit of keeping children away from the table when company comes often leads children to resent the coming of the preacher to the home and to wonder if anything will be left for them to eat. The child's eagerness may even lead him to peep through the dining-room keyhole to see if all of the chicken is gone. It is tragedy for a child to be made to feel in the way at home or at church.

There are parents who actually step in and interpose their will when the child is anxious to take an open

stand for Christ. A deacon in an important Baptist
church once said to me that he did not like to see a boy
join the church before he was fifteen. I replied to him,
that, if the devil kept control of his boy till he was
fifteen and his life habits were formed, the chances were
two to one that he would never be converted. Numer-
ous investigations in scientific pedagogy have shown that
the age of decision for Christ is in the 'teens. The difficulties multiply rapidly after one is twenty-one. The
tree grows the way the twig is bent. In a meeting in a
Baptist church I once saw a father seize his two children
and hinder their coming forward for Christ. One does
not wish his children to take a stand for Christ without
surrender to Christ. But in the case of the normal child
with adequate instruction, it is a simple matter to yield
the heart to Jesus as Lord and Saviour. I have seen
some tragic cases in my own town when children were
prevented from joining the church. They never did and
their lives counted for nothing as far as Christianity
was concerned. They were pushed back when they
started toward Christ. It is a terrible blunder to make.
I once knew a father who under the influence of his
faith-healing had refused to allow anti-toxin to be given
to his two little boys who had diphtheria. As a result
they both died, and the father was responsible for their
death. What about parents who keep their children
away from Christ?

There are tragedies enough in spite of all we can do.
Parents, teachers, preachers all make blunders without
number because of ignorance. These are sad indeed, but
far more lamentable is it when one deliberately shuts
the door in the face of a young heart that is eagerly
turning to Christ. It is not certain whether by " these
little ones " (Luke 17: 2) Jesus means all his followers
or just little children, or those young in the faith. " To
lead even one astray is an awful responsibility " (Plummer). Jesus says: " It were well for him if a millstone

were hanged about his neck, and he were thrown into the sea, rather than that he should cause one of these little ones to stumble." There have always been men and women who set pitfalls for the young to entice them into sin, to initiate them into the ways of vice. Paul pictures such creatures in Romans 1: 32. In the old days of the saloon at a convention of saloon-keepers in Ohio it was deliberately proposed that they should invite the boys in and give them free drinks so as to train up drunkards for their business. " Nickels spent in treating of boys will come back to you in dollars." Recently liquor journals in New York City have carried advertisements to the effect that, if beer is to have a proper sale, boys and young men must be taught the taste of beer which they no longer have because of prohibition which did not prohibit. Boys and girls at every turn are the victims of evil men and women who seek to lead them astray.

4. Demanding a Chance for the Children.

This Jesus demanded then, and he demands it of us now. " Whosoever shall receive this little child in my name receiveth me " (Luke 9: 48). In Mark (9: 37) we have " one of such little children " and in Matthew (18: 5) " one such little child." Jesus had taken this little child in Peter's house in his arms and then placed it by his side as he sought to teach the apostles the greatness of service rather than the greatness of rank or position. Jesus does not consider the child a nuisance or in the way, but as in the very center of things, in the midst of family life, and of kingdom work. We catch a glimpse of the glory of Christ's own childhood in Luke's Gospel, how " the child grew, and waxed strong, filled with wisdom; and the grace of God was upon him " (2: 40). As a child he had the habit of going to the synagogue in Nazareth (Luke 4: 16). When twelve years old Joseph and Mary took the boy Jesus on a visit to the passover feast in Jerusalem and accidentally left him behind in the city. They found him sitting in the temple, "sitting in the midst of the doctors, both hearing them and asking them questions" (Luke 2: 46), this most gifted and wonderful of all children, eager to talk about the deepest things in his own life, the dawning of the Messianic consciousness in his own heart. He could only wonder that Joseph and Mary did not know where alone he could be: "Wist ye not that I must be in my Father's house?" So Jesus "advanced in wisdom and stature, and in favour with God and men" (Luke 2: 52). The human environment of our Lord's childhood seems limited enough according to modern standards. But he had a pious mother who opened to him the Scriptures and gave him an atmosphere of love, sympathy, and the highest hopes, sustained as she was by the words of the angel Gabriel, of the shepherds, and of Simeon and Anna, all of which she cherished in her heart. The boy Jesus found friends with other children, with birds of the air, and the flowers of the fields, and his soul moved in growing fellowship with his Father in heaven who was guiding him to his destiny.

It is folly for parents to neglect the spiritual life of the child. In our complex civilization the public schools in spite of great advances in education do but little for the moral training of the children and practically nothing for the spiritual uplift of children who get no help at home and often every hindrance. It is not only in the slum districts of our cities where the children run in the streets and alleys and learn the ways and works of the devil. Many respectable homes or apartments are practically godless and sometimes have an atheistic atmosphere. No religious journals enter it. No religious books are found there. No family worship is held and even grace is omitted at the meals. No preacher comes into the home, and if he does, personal religious conversation is taboo. The child reared in such an atmosphere is ushered into a life of worldliness and pleasure. Self-indulgence instead of self-culture and service to God and man is the motivating influence of a life of jazz, radio, movies, and finally wild parties. The greatest business in the world is not making money, but making men. Human life is worth more than dollars. Babies are more of an ornament to a wife than poodle dogs. Boys and girls reared in the nurture and admonition of the Lord are the stars in the crown of fathers and mothers. Give the child a decent chance to be a child of God. Jesus calls for and welcomes the child. The Bolsheviki hope to win the children to atheism and so to dislodge Christ in Russia. There is a definite atheistic propaganda going on in our own land to win the youth to atheism. It is folly to sit idly by and let the children slip through our fingers to ruin. The Roman Catholic priest claims that, if he can train the child for seven years, no one can undo what he has taught by that time. Give Christ a chance with your child while there is time. It will soon be too late. If the child is father of the man, it is important to start him right.

5. *Jesus Making the Child a Type for Grown People.*

To most grown persons this language seems to be a complete reversal of the facts of life. Many people regard the child as an empty mould for receiving the ideas of adults. That is not the idea of Jesus. The child is a model for believers in his simple trust. " Whosoever shall not receive the kingdom of heaven as a little child, shall in no wise enter therein " (Mark 10:15). Jesus does not here say or mean what some modern theologians hold, that the child is already in the kingdom of God and simply has to remain in it (a complete denial of natural and inherited sin and of the need of regeneration for salvation). The salvation of children dying in infancy before the age of responsibility is quite another matter and is amply provided for by the grace of God through the atoning death of Christ (Rom. 5: 13f.). The whole point of Christ's use of the child as a model for adults in the matter of receiving the kingdom lies in the fact of the simple trust of the child in just giving his whole heart to God. The kingdom of God is, in fact, composed of precisely those who accept Christ as Saviour and enter into God's kingdom in this genuine way. Jesus does not mean by his words, " for of such is the kingdom of God," that only children or that all children, are in the kingdom of heaven. He means that all who are in the kingdom enter as children do with simple and sincere trust. The normal child in an atmosphere of love is not suspicious, but trustful. " The child receives what is offered to it, in full trust that it is good for it " (Plummer). We make ourselves models for children, but Jesus makes the children models for us on this point of believing. The Master by no means implies that children are sinless, perfect, and need no correction and no training, after the fad of some modern psychologists who leave children to grow up wild and undisciplined. " Except ye turn, and become as little children, ye shall in no wise enter into the kingdom of heaven " (Matt. 18: 3). " It is not these children, not all children, but those who are childlike in character, especially in humility and trustfulness, who are best fitted for the kingdom " (Plummer.)

It is an utter mistake to make children feel that they are absolutely perfect, just as it is a crime to treat them as if they are imps of perdition. Every reader of *Nicholis Nickleby* and of *Jane Eyre* knows what are the heartaches and the heartbreaks of lonely and unappreciated children at home and in school. Happy are those who bring the children to Jesus for his blessing and for his love. Christ is calling still for the children that they may have a chance to come to him. The answer to that call will decide the future of the world for weal or for woe.

V

AARON THE COMPROMISER

"And Aaron spake all the words which the Lord had spoken unto Moses, and did the signs in the sight of the people."
—EXODUS 4: 30.

AARON'S light is dimmed by the brighter light of Moses, his brother, to such an extent that many fail to catch the full stature of the man and of his ministry. The lesser lights fare badly in the presence of the greater—the moon before the sun. Just as Moses was the great lawgiver for Israel, so Aaron was the founder of the priestly line that lasted till the destruction of the temple and the city of Jerusalem by Titus in A. D. 70. Aaron came to wear "the holy garments" of the priest in ministering unto the Lord (Ex. 39: 1; 40: 13). That great Aaronic line of priests became one of the glories of Israel to be finally surpassed and rendered useless by the greater priesthood of Jesus Christ after the order of Melchizedek (Heb. 7: 1–28).

1. Aaron the Mouthpiece of Moses.

Moses was slow of speech, according to his own confession, so that the Lord chose Aaron to be a mouth to Moses. "Thou shalt speak unto him, and put the words in his mouth: and I will be with thy mouth, and will teach you what ye shall do. And he shall be thy spokesman unto the people" (Ex. 4: 15f.). Clearly Moses is the Lord's chosen instrument for leading the people of Israel out of their bondage in Egypt. As a matter of fact, Moses was too humble, and the anger of God was kindled against him for his reluctance to do God's will.

So Moses needed Aaron, who was especially chosen to play a secondary rôle in the great undertaking. Moses was the prophet to whom God spoke directly and Aaron received the will of God indirectly through Moses. The task of Aaron was to interpret God's will to the people in such a way that they would understand it and heed it. Moses was the source of the wisdom of God for Aaron, while Aaron was the orator to deliver it to the people. It was an honourable post for Aaron, but a distinctly secondary one. But Aaron was glad in his heart (Ex. 4: 14) to serve God and to help Moses in this humble position. "He went and met him in the mountain of God and kissed him" (Ex. 4: 27) and he carried out the compact obediently and circumspectly in the main. Moses was the prophet of God, while Aaron was the prophet of Moses. Aaron was formally acknowledged to be only a second-fiddle to Moses. In that capacity he did well. The only time he played first fiddle, he played the fool. That was when the people asked for gods to go before them because Moses tarried in the mountain with God. The majority of us have to occupy subordinate positions in life and so the case of Aaron should interest us. Aaron was a satellite of Moses and for that reason it is not always easy to separate their personalities and their tasks. Aaron did not possess the great gifts that stand out so sharply in Moses.

2. Helpfulness in Coöperating with Moses.

In this capacity we see Aaron at his best. It is the most striking element in his character. He is a man who "can speak well" (Ex. 4: 14). That is a gift worth having and has marked out many a man since as a preacher of the gospel. There was no nobler thing for Aaron to do with his oratory than to help Moses deliver the Israelites from the bondage in Egypt. Silas was not lowered by helping Paul, nor John Mark by being Peter's interpreter, nor Melanchthon by giving his scholarship to Martin Luther's fight in the Reformation. The spirit of coöperation is needed in family, church, and state to counteract too much individualism and to prevent the tyranny of bolshevism. The spirit of helpfulness is opposed to selfishness which is the fountain of all sin.

In the contest with Pharaoh in Egypt Moses would tell Aaron to take the rod and strike it over the waters of Egypt so that the water became blood. Then the frogs came up. Aaron smote the dust and lice came upon man and beast. The flies came. The cattle died of murrain. Boils came upon man and beast. Hail devastated the land. The locusts ate up all that was left. The darkness came. Finally the firstborn in every home was taken save the homes of Israel where blood was sprinkled upon the doorpost. Then Pharaoh yielded and the people escaped and his hosts perished in the Red Sea.

But it was at Rephidim that the people were ready to stone Moses because they had no water to drink. Water was given out of the rock, but Amalek attacked Israel at this crisis. Moses took Aaron and Hur with him to the top of the hill to pray while Joshua fought Amalek in the plain. " And it came to pass, when Moses held up his hand, that Israel prevailed; and when he let down his hand, Amalek prevailed " (Ex. 17: 11). That was a dramatic moment, fully appreciated by Moses and Aaron and Hur, whether Joshua and the host of Israel understood it or not. Moses' hands grew heavy so that Aaron and Hur took a stone and put it under Moses while " Aaron and Hur stayed up his hands, the one on the one side, and the other on the other side; and his hands were steady until the going down of the sun " (Ex. 17: 12). As a result, Israel discomfited Amalek that day. Moses did the praying and Joshua did the fighting. Aaron and Hur performed the humble task of holding up the hands of Moses in prayer. This narrative is a parable and a prophecy of many a crisis in church and state through all the centuries. If the officers, not to say every church member, only held up the hands of the pastor while he prayed and preached, what a different story would be told! Often the pastor has to hold up his own hands against the dead weight, or active opposition, of one or more members of the church. In the history of the United States George Washington carried on the war of the Revolution against apathy, criticism, and finally treachery in the case of Benedict Arnold. Abraham Lincoln had men in his cabinet who admitted their superiority to him and were willing to see him sidetracked. In the case of Andrew Johnson there was finally mutiny in his own cabinet and an effort to have him impeached. How is the battle going, brother, in your community? Are you upholding your pastor, or are you pulling hard against him by idle criticisms of his sermons and life? Are you tearing down instead of building? Miss Mulock once heard a labouring man say, as he helped a little girl across the street, when laughed at by onlookers: " Aye, but a 'andful of 'elp is worth a cartload of pity." The squire of Northumberland says (*Chevy Chase*, p. 4):

> " *I wot youe byn great lordes twa,*
> *I am a poor sauyar of lande;*
> *I wyll never see my captaine fyght on a fylde,*
> *And stande my-selffe and looke on,*
> *But whyle I may my weppone welde,*
> *I wyll not fayl both harte and hande.*"

That is the spirit of coöperative helpfulness seen in Aaron.

3. And Yet Aaron Yielded to the Clamour of the People in the Absence of Moses.

There are few sadder stories than the failure of Aaron to hold the people of Israel to the worship of God during the forty days while Moses was on Mount Sinai receiving the tables of the covenant from God. They had murmured already often about the food and the water. But when Moses delayed to come down, the people said to Aaron: "Up, make us gods, which shall go before us; for as for this Moses, the man that brought us up out of Egypt, we know not what is become of him" (Ex. 32: 1). It is the old story, out of sight, out of mind. The Israelites recognize that Moses did bring them out of Egypt, but they are still in the wilderness, and they have given up Moses as lost. The people are clearly ignorant and unable to conceive of worship of God without some idolatrous symbol such as the people in Egypt had for their gods. Here was Aaron's great opportunity such as comes to many a man once. If eloquence was ever needed, it was now. But, like many a preacher or politician since that day, Aaron temporized with the people and encouraged their restless doubt. He became a follower of the rabble, instead of becoming a leader of the multitude. He put his ear to the ground to hear the rumblings of the groundling instead of lifting up his voice to sound a bugle note of loyalty to God. He now stood in the place of Moses, but acted the part of a coward. He was more concerned with his own popularity with the mob than with his loyalty to God. *Vox populi* is only *vox dei* when it is the echo of God's voice. In this case, as often, it was clearly *vox diaboli*.

Aaron did not say in so many words that he would make idols for the people to worship, but he implied it. He asked for their gold, for their earrings and other trinkets, "and fashioned it with a graving tool, and made it a molten calf" (Ex. 32: 4); this did Aaron, the priest of God, clad in his holy garments. The people cried in their glee: "These are thy gods, O Israel, which brought thee up out of the land of Egypt." Aaron timidly said: "To-morrow shall be a feast to the Lord," as if in worshipping Aaron's golden calf they were really worshipping God. Even now men dethrone Christ as

Lord and Saviour, rob him of his deity, set up golden
calves of Theosophy, Spiritualism, Christian Science, Humanism, Buddhism, Mahometanism, and solemnly proclaim a feast unto the Lord.

It is pitiful and pathetic to see the poor figure that
Aaron makes before the wrath of Moses when he at
length does come down from Mount Sinai. He flung the
two tables of the testimony to one side when he saw the
people dancing around the golden calf in their frenzied
worship. He challenged Aaron hotly: "What did this
people unto thee that thou hast brought a great sin upon
them" (Ex. 32: 21). Aaron weakly apologized: "Thou
knowest the people, that they are set on evil." He explained feebly that he asked for their gold. "I cast it
into the fire, and there came out this calf" (Ex. 32: 24),
as if by accident and not fashioned by Aaron himself
on purpose to please the people. Poor Aaron overlooks
the fact that, in the absence of Moses, he was the only
leader that the people had to hold them true to God.
And here he is blaming the people and excusing his own
treason. "Like people like priest." Alas, yes, too often,
but it is also true that "like priest like people." If the
preacher holds forth "the truth as it is in Jesus," the
people are likely to remain firm in the faith of the fathers.

We read that Moses turned in disgust from Aaron and
stood in the gate of the camp and cried: "Whoso is on
the Lord's side, let him come unto me" (Ex. 32: 25).
The sons of Levi came and Moses demanded that they
consecrate themselves to God "that he may bestow upon
you a blessing this day." Three thousand of the people
were slain because of this great sin wrought by Aaron's
cowardice. Moses made a plea for God to blot him out
of his book and spare the people, but "God smote the
people because they made the calf which Aaron made"
(Ex. 32: 35). Both Aaron and the people made the
golden calf, joint responsibility. The golden calf was

ground into powder and the people had to drink it. There is always punishment for pastor and people when they disobey God and go astray. In every crisis the leaders need to thunder like Moses for volunteers: " Who is on the Lord's side? " There are always some brave-hearted and clear-visioned souls who will take their stand out in the open for Christ who is the only hope of the world. It was a great moment at the World's Fair in Chicago in 1893 at the Congress of Religions when Joseph Cook, of Boston, as champion of Christ, de-manded what else save the blood of Christ could wash away the stain from Lady Macbeth's bloody hand. The blood of Jesus Christ alone can do that.

4. And Aaron Along with Miriam Finally Grew En-vious of Moses.

Perhaps it was inevitable that this should come as Aaron developed in his priestly functions and was no longer merely the spokesman of Moses. Besides, Mir-iam, the sister of Moses and Aaron, had gifts of her own in song and prophecy. Moses had angered her by marry-ing another wife, a Cushite woman whom both Aaron and Miriam disliked. So then one day they spoke out to each other what had slumbered within them for long: " Hath the Lord spoken only with Moses? Hath he not spoken also with us? " (Num. 12: 2). But God heard their jealous talk and suddenly spoke to all three (Moses, Aaron, and Miriam) out of the pillar of cloud (Num. 12: 5). And Miriam became a leper and Aaron was cut to the heart, for he also was guilty, though Miriam had probably stimulated his envy. God spared Miriam, but it was a needed lesson for both, and it is a warning to every jealous preacher. Aaron was three years older than Moses and Miriam had watched Moses while he was a babe in the ark by the river Nile. Aaron was also more gifted in speech than Moses. What spe-cious arguments envy and jealousy can weave to ensnare our souls. These slimy serpents creep into the hearts of the servants of the Lord. "I am weary of hearing Aristides called the just," said a man at Athens who argued for his banishment. God heard the jealous talk of Aaron and Miriam and he hears it to-day wherever and whenever it occurs. This sin was like a boomerang for Miriam and Aaron. There is a story of a Greek wrestler who grew envious of a statue in honour of a rival. He pulled it down and it fell on his own head and killed him. Envy stings most the one who is subject to it.

5. *We See Aaron Silent in Sorrow.*

He had his share of sin, as we have seen, and also his share of sorrow as we all have. Part of Aaron's sorrow came from two of his sons (Nadab and Abihu). They offered "strange fire before the Lord, which he had not commanded them. And there came forth fire from before the Lord, and devoured them, and they died before the Lord" (Lev. 10: 1f.). It was sacrilege on the part of those who knew better. What the two sons did was clearly associated with the idolatrous worship which had been forbidden. The record is very brief but it is possible that these two young men felt that they were merely experimenting with a harmless prank, not worse at any rate than the golden calf that Aaron made. But they reckoned wrongly and a terrible lesson was taught the people by this severe penalty upon the young priests. Moses saw a lesson in the calamity for Aaron and said: "This is it that the Lord spake, saying, I will be sanctified in them that come nigh me, and before all the people I will be glorified." This interpretation of the incident seems obvious enough. It is not always so easy for us to read the meaning of what happens to us; not yet, but some day it will be plainer even to us. We have only this comment further: "And Aaron held his peace." Perhaps Aaron had failed in teaching reverence

to these two sons. Who knows? " I was dumb, I
opened not my mouth because thou didst it " (Ps. 39: 9).
Another pleasing incident to Aaron's credit follows: In
the midst of the plague that followed the rebellion of
Korah we read that Aaron, under the direction of Moses,
took his censer as high priest " and stood between the
dead and the living; and the plague was stayed "
(Num. 16: 48).

Miriam died at Kadesh (Num. 20: 1). Both Moses
and Aaron were kept out of the Promised Land because
of their disobedience in smiting the rock the second time
instead of speaking to it this time as the Lord commanded. " Because ye believed not in me, to sanctify
me in the eyes of the children of Israel, therefore ye
shall not bring this assembly into the land which I have
given them " (Num. 20: 12).

One day Moses, Aaron, and Eleazar (his son) went
up on Mount Hor. Moses there took off the holy
priestly garments from Aaron and put them upon
Eleazar. " And Aaron died there on the top of the
mount " (Num. 20: 28). He was 123 years old.
Moses and Eleazar came down without Aaron. He was
a noble man and servant of God, with the faults of his
qualities, but a real helper of Moses in bringing a re-
bellious people from Egypt to Canaan.

VI

CHRIST'S SCHOOL ADVERTISEMENT

"Take my yoke upon you and learn from me."
—MATTHEW 11: 29.

THE words of the text occur only in Matthew, but verses 25 to 27 occur almost verbatim in Luke 10: 21 and 22 in another connection. There is no difficulty at all in thinking that Jesus repeated them on two different occasions, here after the denunciation of the cities of privilege (Chorazin, Bethsaida, Capernaum) for their failure to receive Christ, there upon the return of the seventy from their preaching and healing tour.[1] The words of the text are among "the special treasures of the First Gospel" (Plummer). The use of yoke (*zugon*) as a metaphor for teaching was proverbial with the Jews in their writings like "the yoke of the law," "the yoke of the kingdom of heaven."

So in Acts 15: 10 Peter objects to putting the yoke of the Jewish law upon the neck of the disciples and Paul in Galatians 5: 1 calls it "a yoke of bondage." In the *Didache* or *Teaching of the Twelve* we have "the whole yoke of the law." So in Sirach 51: 25 Wisdom says: "Put your neck under the yoke, and let your soul receive

---

[1] This "ærolite from the Johannean heaven" (Hase) is not simply quoted by the *Logia of Jesus*, the Q of criticism (the non-Marcan portions of Matthew and Luke, the oldest known Gospel document), but the use of "the Father, the Son" in this high sense so common in John's Gospel, appears also in the Gospel of Mark, the earliest of our Four Gospels (Mark 13: 32; Matthew 24: 36). Even Schmiedel regards the language here an original utterance by Jesus. Plummer considers the rejection of this saying as genuine to be "reckless criticism" based "not upon critical principles, but upon prejudices."

instruction." Such language (Broadus) "is only a figurative way of saying, 'Become my pupils (disciples), submit yourselves to my instruction.'" Yoke is the Hebrew metaphor for "school" as it is regarded to-day by many pupils. Our English word "school," however, is Greek (*scholē*) and means leisure. We have one example of this Greek word for school in the New Testament in Acts 19: 10 as Paul was "discoursing daily in the school of Tyrannus." The Greek word did not mean a place of idleness as some pupils treat it, but a place where there was opportunity for study and for scholarly pursuits. In April, 1905, as the cab-driver drove me to my boarding place in Oxford where I was to work for some months in the Bodleian Library, I asked him if the students were in Oxford. "No," he replied, "they have gone down to work." I asked him please to explain his language. He meant, he said, that at Oxford they played cricket, drank tea, rowed on the Isis, and in the vacation time went home to read, and study. That was simply the cab-driver's interpretation of "school." But Jesus employs naturally the Hebrew metaphor and is here giving an urgent appeal for pupils to come to his school and learn from him, the Greatest Teacher of all time. The arguments presented by the Master apply to us to-day, as well as to those who first heard him speak. Keim calls this passage "this pearl of the sayings of Jesus." What are Christ's reasons for coming to his school?

1. *Because a Specialist Is in Charge of It.*

Jesus claims here to be the expert on the knowledge of God. Only the Father fully knows the Son. No one except the Son fully knows the Father. The Son alone by a divine gift knows the Father's nature and the relation of the Son to the Father. Jesus here claims that "all things have been delivered unto me by my Father" (verse 27) in language like that on the mountain in

Galilee before the Ascension (Matt. 28: 18). " Jesus is the authorized instructor in the knowledge of God " (Broadus). This is a familiar idea in the Gospel of John (5: 18–47) where Jesus claims equality with the Father in nature, knowledge and power. " All things whatsoever the Father hath are mine: therefore said I, that he taketh of mine, and shall declare it unto you " (John 16: 15). So Jesus plainly says to Philip: " He that hath seen me hath seen the Father " (John 14: 9). This is the day of experts and Jesus is the only way to true knowledge of God. That is the plain meaning of the language in Matthew 11: 27 and Luke 10: 22. The great words to Thomas in John 14: 6 occur to us here: " I am the way, and the truth, and the life. No one cometh unto the Father, but by me." Jesus does not here stand on a platform with Confucius, with Buddha, with Mahomet. He stands alone as the one who can show us the way to God. Peter did not flinch on this point as he faced the Sanhedrin, the expert builders who had rejected Jesus whom God made the head of the corner in his temple: " And in none other is there salvation: for neither is there any other name under heaven, that is given among men, wherein we must be saved " (Acts 4: 12). Men are still trying to be saved in other ways, but without Christ they are still without hope and without God in the world (Eph. 2: 12).

Come to my school, then, says Jesus, for I alone can tell you what you need to know about God. " Neither does any know the Father, save the Son, and he to whomsoever the Son wills to reveal him." Jesus has the power to reveal the Father. He is the supreme Interpreter of God to men since he came to us from the bosom of the Father (John 1: 18). It is an idle waste of time and energy for men to seek to find God by mere speculative philosophy or by scientific research. God is spirit and Jesus touches our spirits with God's Spirit and so we come to know him. There is a step for us to take, to be sure, the obedience to the will of God that opens the door of the heart to God's Spirit: "If any man wills to do his will, he shall know of the teaching" (John 7: 17).

Jesus is the one Teacher in the university of God. It is a case of Mark Hopkins on one end of the log and the boy on the other. That is a real college. Broadus used to say that a modern school required four B's: brains, boys, books, and buildings. And in this order, for brains in the teacher ranks first. Socrates, Plato, Aristotle,—each was a school in himself. Aristotle taught Alexander and the world was turned around. Jesus taught Paul and the world was turned upside down and we are still living in the world made by Paul on the work of Alexander and Julius Cæsar. There were other teachers of mystical religion in that age, but they have all vanished in the limbo of the past (the Eleusinian mysteries, the worship of Isis, of Cybele, of Mithra) save as they reappear in modern evanescent mist and fog like Theosophy, Bahaism, Christian Science, Humanism. Abraham, Moses, David, Elijah, Isaiah, all had high experiences with God, but here is one who speaks a language unlike any ever heard before. The self-consciousness of Jesus as the Son of God in a sense not true of others confronts us here. He pleads for pupils to come to his school to learn from him directly what he has to tell them about the Father. He is competent and he knows how to show us the Father. He is the expert on the greatest theme that can occupy the mind of man, who is made in the image of God.

2. *Come to My Shcool, says Jesus, Because It Is for the Plodders and the Puzzled.*

"Come unto me, all ye that labour and are heavy laden" (Matt. 11: 28). There is a sublime majesty in these words from the carpenter of Nazareth, the Galilean peasant prophet, unschooled by the rabbis, taught by his Father, and so able to do what the rabbis could not do, show men the will of God. " He stands as the Great Teacher who alone can give true, saving knowledge of God " (Broadus). At another time Jesus says of the rabbis, the accepted teachers of the current Pharisaic Judaism: " They bind heavy burdens and grievous to be borne, and lay them on men's shoulders; but they themselves will not move them with their finger " (Matt. 23: 4). It is a severe indictment against the preachers of the time. In contrast to these religious teachers Jesus invites those toiling under the rabbinical yoke to bring this and all other burdens to him. The yoke which Peter said " neither our fathers nor we were able to bear " (Acts 15: 10). " Bring me your burdens," pleads Jesus. In his first sermon in Nazareth Jesus applied Isaiah 61: 1f. as fulfilled in his mission. He was anointed to preach glad tidings to the poor, to proclaim release to the captives, and recovering of sight to the blind, to set at liberty the bruised, to proclaim the acceptable year of the Lord. That message fascinated at first the hearers in Nazareth who yet wondered how he, a fellow-citizen of theirs, could do these glorious deeds.

The best teacher is the one who helps the pupil to solve the problems in his lessons till he masters them. School children have real problems. The wise mother loves for the child to bring his problems to her. He is sure of sympathy and understanding from her. In my college life I have a vivid remembrance of a problem in oblique-angled spherical trigonometry that puzzled me for a couple of days before I solved it. Jesus asks all the slow and dull pupils to come to his school. I have known only one school that advertised for dunderheads. Possibly plenty of them come anyhow. This school was taught for boys who had difficulty in making the entrance examinations to colleges and universities. The principal boasted that no pupil that he trained ever failed to make the required grade in the best American universities.

Young Theodore Roosevelt was considered by some a blockhead in school because he asked so many questions. He wanted to understand the point at issue. Schools must have high standards of scholarship and Jesus is not lowering his ideals and is not approving lazy dullards. On the contrary he severely rebuked the Twelve Apostles for their dullness in not understanding his teaching about the leaven of the Pharisees, the Sadducees, and Herod (Mark 8: 14–21). But the Master offers sympathy and his own supreme knowledge in solving the grave and great problems of human life. Often the best thing done by the physician is to listen kindly as the patient tells his woes.

3. Come to My School, says Jesus, Because Even Babes Can Learn in It.

He thanks his Father " that thou didst hide these things from the wise and the understanding and didst reveal them unto babes " (Matt. 11: 25; Luke 10: 21). Jesus thanks God both for hiding from the intelligentsia and for making it plain for babes. This paradox can be easily misunderstood. Jesus is not placing a premium on ignorance or obscurantism. Gilbert K. Chesterton, who is fond of paradoxes himself, recently said that what surprised him on a recent visit to the United States was the ignorance of the educated. There are learned fools who are confused by the lumber of learning and are unable to see the reality because of the rubbish and clatter of things. They cannot see the wood for the trees. Paul noted that in Corinth " not many wise after the flesh, not many mighty, not many noble were called " (1 Cor. 1: 26), though some were. Most men are not intellectual giants, do not possess great wealth or high station and great power, do not have a proud ancestry. Many of the greatest have always been drawn to Christ, but it is the glory of Christ that he appeals to the common man and makes him an uncommon man. Here he thanks his Father that intellectual wisdom is not necessary for the recognition of the Divine Wisdom. He does not mean that intellectual power is a barrier to the reception of the Gospel; but it is immaterial: all that is required is childlike simplicity. " Ignorance is no qualification, intellect is no disqualification " (Plummer). What Jesus requires is the simplicity and directness of children. It is a joy to preach to children, if one is willing to use simple words and short sentences, speak directly to the point and quit. I have always observed that, when the children understood a sermon, the adults were able to do so. There are a good many reasons why sermons may be dull. Some are really dull, but others are so because they are not understood. " Not all men can become wise and intelligent, but all may, by the grace of God become babes (comp. 1 Cor. 3: 18). The most useful Christians will be those who are ' wise and intelligent ' and are also ' babes '—intellectual and cultivated as possible, but childlike in spirit " (Broadus). Jesus will rebuke the stupidity of the rabbis in the temple when they showed resentment at the praise of Jesus by the boys who hailed him as the Messiah (Matt. 21: 16). Out of the mouth of babes and sucklings God has perfected praise (Ps. 8: 2).

4. Come to My School, says Jesus, Because of the Gentleness of the Teacher.

" For I am meek and lowly in heart " (Matt. 11: 29). Paul entreats the Corinthians " by the meekness and gentleness of Christ " (2 Cor. 10: 1) to try to understand him who was also lowly while among them. Paul was of a fiery disposition and could explode on occasion like James and John, the Sons of Thunder. John came to be called the Apostle of Love after he mastered his spirit. But Paul and John on occasion let loose their indignation as Jesus did in Matthew 23 against the hypocrisy of the Pharisees who were plotting his death.

Yet Jesus is the perfect example of meekness. " To learn gentleness from Him is to win a Beatitude " (McNeile). The ancients did not praise meekness or humility. They were actually considered by many vices, not virtues. Moses was called a meek man and yet Moses was not allowed to enter the Promised Land because of an explosion of pride and anger. Jesus does not mention his own meekness and humility in heart in order to boast, but simply to encourage people to come close to him and learn from him. Teachers are sometimes regarded as harsh and unfeeling. The earnestness of the teacher is not always understood. He repeats and explains and turns the thing round and round. Students do not always appreciate the patience of the teacher in his effort to make the subject plain. Some teachers are severe and repellent. It is not always easy to preserve an open mind and have patience between student and teacher. I may be allowed to say that I have often been told by my old students, whom I have always loved: " We all love you now, Dr. Bob," with the emphasis on the " now." I loved them " then " as well as " now." But, however imperfect we teachers are, and James (3: 1) confesses that all teachers stumble in speech, there is no imperfection in Christ. He is the only perfect teacher. He is always gentle in heart, not in mere appearance or for professional courtesy. " I am lowly in heart, notwithstanding that I have borne witness to myself as the Son of the Father " (Stier).

5. *Come to My School, says Jesus, Because of the Refreshment to Your Soul in It.*

" Come and I will refresh you," he says. Then he repeats: " And ye shall find refreshment for your souls." The Greek word (*ana-pauō*) is very common and means literally to cause to rest again (" to rest up " in our vernacular) after toil and weariness. So Jesus invited the apostles, after their return from the preaching and healing tour of Galilee: "Come ye apart to a desert place and refresh yourselves a bit" (Mark 6: 31). The word is used of the blessed rest of the dead "that they may rest (be refreshed) from their toils" (Rev. 14: 13). So here Jesus, as the supreme teacher, promises tranquillity of soul and refreshment of spirit, rejuvenation of the personality. "I will refresh you," he says, "and ye shall find refreshment." We have a part to play in it also. "All religions profess to give rest for the spirit. Christianity alone can truly fulfil the promise" (Broadus). Christ is the Rejuvenator of tired men and women. Try him with your troubles, ye weary and worn souls. With Christ you have a new outlook on life and you see that life with him is worth while. No Christian in his senses commits suicide. That is the logic of the defeated Stoic or the sated Epicurean, to commit *hari-kari* is not patriotism and it is not piety. There is unending intellectual stimulus with Jesus. Give him your soul and you will thus find it in fulness of joy and power (Matt. 10: 39). Then you will learn that he is life. "Whosoever drinks of the water that I shall give him will never thirst, but the water that I shall give him will become in him a fountain of water leaping up into eternal life" (John 4: 14). The words of Jesus here are beyond the inventions of man and are addressed to the whole race for all time (Plummer). The one who understands Christ here "has found his way to the heart of Christianity" (William Sanday). The words of Jesus are spirit and life (John 6: 63) in a sense true of no other words ever spoken or heard. The Father spoke words of approval on the Mount of Transfiguration and said: "Hear ye him" (Mark 9: 7; Matt. 17: 5; Luke 9: 35). The Greek New Testament, just because it gives us the words of Jesus, is worth more than all other books in all the world through all time.

*6. Come to My School, says Jesus, Because in Time
    My Yoke Is Easy and the Burden Light.*

Not at first, but all the same "take my yoke upon
you." It is necessary for discipline and for service. The
ox has to be harnessed to the yoke if he is to learn to
pull with his yoke-fellow, otherwise the load will never
be drawn. The young ox, like the young colt, resists at
first, but finally submits. For a while the two oxen
may pull in opposite directions, like some church members, but gradually they get used to the yoke, like
married people, and become actually happy in the yoke.
There are those to-day who clamour for the abolition
of all laws, rules, restrictions, inhibitions, prohibitions,
and advocate absolute freedom as if we were like Robin-
son Crusoe on a desert island. But a city with no
government, no mayor, no officers, no police, no traffic
regulations, no punishment for crime, would be at the
mercy of gangsters and bandits and no sensible people
would live in it. A family without a head and without
love would be anarchy. A church with no pastor, no
officers, no Bible, no ideals, would be a mob. A school
with no teachers, no lessons, no examinations, would be
a farce. Jesus has his yoke and offers it to us all. It
is folly to talk about a gospel with no principles, no
creed, no message. There are rules in Christ's school.
You must come to his school on Christ's own terms.
You must take him as Master, as Lord, as Saviour
from sin. He is the Teacher about God, about man,
about sin and salvation. He offers himself as the
Redeemer. Will you enroll in Christ's school, and now?

Christ does not promise you idleness and ease. He
offers you a life of burden bearing and of service. The
yoke you must wear to the end. But you will come to
rejoice in the yoke as a privilege and the badge of
service. The burden will grow lighter with the years.
The word here for "light" in Greek (*chrēstos*) means
both kind and useful or good. It is a "yoke that does

not gall the neck, nor cramp so as to hinder the draw-
ing " (Broadus). God's commands are precise and not
mere platitudes, but they are not " heavy " (1 John 5: 3)
to the one who knows the love of Jesus, his Teacher.
The ideals of Christ as Teacher rise far above those of
all other teachers through the ages, " but Christ's yoke,
in proportion as it is accepted, gives the buoyancy and
life which enable men to meet His much greater demands " (McNeile). The pupil of Jesus finds joy in the
lessons, in the tests, in the examinations that come from
him. Many are charmed for a moment by new and
strange voices that offer surcease for the soul that is
sick with sin. But it is the voice of some siren. It is
a flickering will-o'-the-wisp, not the Light of the world.
Jesus is still standing with outstretched hand and is
inviting all the tired and troubled of earth to come to
his school. He challenges the young men and maidens,
in and out of school, to come to his school, the university of the soul, the school for the whole man, the college
of eternity.

VII

BURDEN-BEARING

"Bear ye one another's burdens, and so fulfil the law of Christ."—GALATIANS 6: 2.

THIS is a good text for hard times when so many who live on the border line of want drop below the line and are in dire need. But there are always many who carry heavy burdens, some with aching hearts and smiling faces. And there are always some slackers, dodgers, deserters, traitors whose real character is brought out in times of trial like war. Lightfoot thinks that Paul wrote the Epistle to the Galatians from Corinth just after his arrival and the settling of the grave situation there. These verses (1–10) carry a message for us all to-day as we face our own problems and those of others.

1. *If a Man Be Overtaken in a Slip.*

It is a condition of the second class, a supposed and possible case, that Paul presents. The tone is like that in 2 Corinthians 2: 6–8 toward the offender in Corinth who has been punished and has changed his conduct. The word for " overtaken " means literally " to take beforehand " as in 1 Corinthians 11: 21 when one at the Lord's Supper greedily takes the supper before the others. It is also used of Mary of Bethany who anticipated the anointing of Jesus for his burial (Mark 14: 8). Here it means to forestall a man before he can flee, by catching him in his slip or sin. He is surprised and detected in *flagrante delicto*. He is caught in the very act. In a papyrus of the second century A. D. the word is em-

72

ployed of a girl against whom a plot is formed, "that you may do something before she is entrapped." Setting snares for boys and girls is an old game of the evil one. The word here for "fault" means falling beside and then aside, to one side, a lapse or deviation from truth or uprightness of conduct. The papyri examples suggest a slip rather than a wilful sin. The Latin rendering "transgression" suggests rather a stepping across which may be deliberate. The same word is the one used by Jesus of our "transgressions" against God and man (Matt. 6: 15). The word "even" before "if" is not to be overlooked, "even if a man be overtaken in a slip," that is, "even if" it is a serious lapse and not a mere accident. Sins of impulse may be due partly to ignorance or surprise when taken unawares and off one's guard. It is hard for a boy to say: "I did not go to it," but it is true sometimes. Even the strong have their weak spots like the heel of Achilles. There are risks in temptation to make any one pause. Jesus, who triumphed over every temptation, warned the apostles: "Pray that ye enter not into temptation" (Luke 22: 40). This the Master urged as he faced the Tempter again in Gethsemane. And yet some people rush heedlessly into temptation. There was a young girl who said that she was kept straight by the blessed memory of her mother. The presence of Christ in the heart is still more powerful.

2. Mending the Broken Brother.

Paul draws his practical conclusion as to what to do with one who is overtaken in a slip, however serious. "Restore such a one." The word "restore" really means "mend" as we see it used in Matthew 4: 21 of James and John "mending their nets." We have it in our word "articulate." The word is used of surgeons setting a bone or joint. "Mend" the broken one. Do not fling him to the scrap-heap or to the junk-pile. Harold Begbie has a remarkable book called *Broken*

Earthenware in which he tells his wonderful experiences in East London in mending broken hearts and patching up broken lives. We see it also in Hugh Redmond's *God in the Slums*. We ought to see it in the work of every church in the world. The law of the jungle rules the wolves which turn and devour one of the pack that falls. But the law of Christ offers love and help, if a man or woman falls. The true church is a life-saving station and every one should know how to give first aid to broken and crushed hearts.

Paul appeals in particular to the spiritual, "you who are spiritual," to spiritual surgeons, forsooth. A lot of bungling work is done in winning the erring to Christ, in healing wounded souls. In the old days, before aseptic surgery, many a surgeon stropped his knife on his boot, in ignorance of the germs of death that he put thus into the wound. There are miracles of modern surgery as a result of Lord Lister's discovery. But it is still true that only the blood of Christ can wash away the stain of sin. The blood of Jesus does cleanse us from all sin (1 John 1: 7). Faith in Christ brings the only serum for a sin-sick soul. The famous Portland Vase was broken into a thousand pieces, and has been mended. Still more wonderful is the new heart in the broken man. Some lives may seem to us past all mending, but let us not despair. It is better, surely, to give Christ a life before it is so wholly shattered.

This mending calls for skill and also for a spirit of gentleness. The true physician learns that his fingers are sensitive and quick to respond to the most delicate touch of nerve or muscle. Do the mending by all means, but do it " in a spirit of meekness." Paul changes from the plural to the singular in the added clause, " looking to thyself, lest thou also be tempted." " Keep an eye on thyself as well as on the stumbling brother." In 2 Thessalonians 3: 15 Paul urges that they admonish an erring one " as a brother." Augustine says: " There is no sin, which any man has done, but another may do the same." A story is told of John Newton that when he saw a drunken man reeling along, he said, " There, but for the grace of God, goes John Newton." " And if they which be so ready to judge and condemn others, would well consider their own sin, they should find the sins of others which are fallen, to be but motes, and their own sins to be great beams " (Martin Luther). The point in church discipline should be not the cleansing of the church roll, but the restoration of the stumbling sinning saint.

3. Easing the Burdens of Others.

There are burdens that are heavy to bear even when one does not stumble into sin. Some who have not fallen by the wayside need a word of cheer and a helping hand. A stitch in time saves nine. Many a fall or slip can be prevented by a steadying hand at the right time. The word for " burden " (baros) is different from the " load " (phortion) in verse 5. It occurs in Acts 15: 28 of the burdens of the Mosaic ceremonial law which were not to be imposed on the Gentile Christians. It occurs in Matthew 20: 12 of " the burdens of the day and the heat " with the same verb (bastazō) that we have here, the verb used of Jesus bearing his cross to Calvary (John 19: 17) and of our bearing our cross after him (Luke 14: 27). In the case of Jesus Simon of Cyrene was impressed by the soldiers to bear the cross for him (Mark 15: 21), apparently as Jesus staggered under the load. But he began " bearing the cross for himself." There are real burdens that are too heavy to be borne alone. These occasions furnish us an opportunity to " fulfil the law of Christ." This is the law of love and we are to fill it to the full. In Romans 15: 1 Paul puts it thus: " We the strong ought to go on bearing the infirmities of the weak."

In our modern cities we have the appeal of the Com-

munity Chest and every church has its own organiza-
tion for the relief of special need. Times of depression
and unemployment, of drought or flood, of epidemic
and death, intensify the demand that is always present.
The early disciples in Jerusalem had to take unusual
measures to meet the situation after Pentecost when
there was a boycott of Christians by Jews (Acts 4: 34–
37). Paul and Barnabas brought a collection for this
purpose from Antioch (Acts 11: 29f.). Later Paul
brought a large contribution from the churches of
Galatia, Asia, Macedonia, and Achaia (Rom. 15: 25–27).
Paul had practised what he is here preaching. Jesus
draws a wonderful picture in Matthew 25: 31–46 of those
who ministered unto him by ministering unto those in
want and of those who failed to serve him by failing to
help the needy.

There are, to be sure, individual cases that make professional appeals of a wholly unworthy nature. That is
one of the advantages of the various organizations in our
cities to which one can refer such cases for investiga-
tion. I recall vividly an old man with a handsome white
beard who accosted me one day on Chestnut Street,
Louisville, with a pathetic story that appealed to me. I
started to give him what he asked, but concluded to
refer him with my card to the Hope Rescue Mission.
He tore up my card and flung it away. A week later
on Main Street the same old man started the identical
story, but stopped when half through with a twinkle in
his eye and said, " I think that I have seen you before."
I told him that he had. But such cases should not be
allowed to dry up the well-spring of helpfulness within
us. We should keep on putting our shoulders under the
burden of a neighbour who has more than he can carry.
That is the spirit of the Good Samaritan as Jesus told
it to the Jewish lawyer who did not love the Samaritans.
The social message of Christianity is by no means the
whole of the gospel, but it is a vital part.

4. Pitiable Pride.

"If any one thinks that he is something, being nothing, he deceives himself." Literally, "he deceives his own mind." Certainly such a conceited man does not deceive any one else, least of all his wife. There is a papyrus example of the substantive used by a wife of her husband. Clearly he did not deceive her. Paul has it in Titus 1: 10 of the Gnostics whom he thus terms "mind-deceivers." It is amazing how easy it is for some people to gull themselves. It is absurd to think of one who is "nothing" (an absolute zero in intellect or character) thinking that he is "something" great. Just so Simon Magus gave it out that he was "some great one" (Acts 8: 9) and the Samaritans took him at his exalted estimate of himself. Paul (1 Tim. 3: 6) warns Timothy against setting apart "a neophyte" for the ministry "lest he be puffed up and fall into the condemnation of the devil." In 1 Timothy 6: 4 he describes the one who does not accept the words of the Lord Jesus Christ as "puffed up, knowing nothing, but sick about questions and wars of words." That is a close parallel to the self-conceit described here. "In Christian morality self-esteem is vanity, and vanity is nothingness. With the Christian it is not I, but the grace of God which is with me" (Lightfoot). But pride, empty pride in particular, goes before a fall. James in 4: 6 quotes Proverbs 3: 34 to the effect that God resists the proud. There have been abundant illustrations of the downfall of the once mighty from the days of Nebuchadnezzar to our own day. He ate grass like an ox, but many more have eaten what we call "humble pie." Napoleon met Waterloo and St. Helena in the end. There are many people of small caliber who make no great pretensions. These excite no such feeling of disgust as do the pretentious preachers who pose as lords of creation. Humility is essential if we are to help others bear their burdens.

5. *Carrying One's Own Load.*

" His own work let each one test," and not pick flaws
in the work of others. The word here used (*dokimazō*)
for testing or proving is the common one for testing the
genuineness of metals. Those who are "infected with
vain glory" (Luther) have no regard for their own
works nor even care whether they have any at all, so
complacent are they in their self-conceit. But they are
quick to find fault with what others do, though they
themselves do nothing. There will be no occasion for
jealous comparison with what others do if we are really
doing something for Christ ourselves. "For each man
shall bear his own load." So the word (*phortion*) should
be translated to distinguish it from "burdens" (*barē*)
of others in verse 2. *Baros* (burden) "points to a load
of which a man may fairly rid himself when occasion
serves; *phortion* to a load which he is expected to bear"
(Lightfoot). *Phortion* is a diminutive of *phortos* and is
used for a soldier's kit, for a traveling man's pack, for
a ship's load (Acts 27: 10). Jesus insisted that his load
which we are to carry is light (Matt. 11: 30). On the
other hand the Pharisees made their loads which they
placed on the shoulders of men "heavy" (*barea*).
Jesus here (Matt. 23: 4) combined both words in describ-
ing the demands of the Pharisees.

But the point on which Paul is here insisting is that
no Christian shall be a dodger of his own duties, a
slacker in his own work, a bluffer about his own task.
He is to play the man, to do a man's part in the world's
work. There is peril in idleness and unemployment
(forced or voluntary). In Christian activities too many
say: "Let George do it," not me. "Ladies first," lazy
men affirm as in courtesy. We may be bluffers with men,
but not with God who knows full well what we really
are and what we really do. The African word "tote"
very well expresses Paul's idea here. "Let each one
tote his own load." If one falls under the load, there

will more likely be some to come to one's aid. The man who refuses to pick up his own load and to carry on receives little sympathy and less help.

6. Spiritual Commerce.

" But let him that is taught in the word communicate unto him that teacheth in all good things " (verse 6). Lightfoot's paraphrase is pertinent: " I spoke of bearing one another's burdens. There is one special application I would make of this rule. Provide for the temporal wants of your teachers in Christ." The word here for " is taught " (*katēcheō*) is a late one which means to sound or echo down upon, to teach orally, to instruct (Luke 1: 4; Acts 18: 25). The papyri use it for legal instruction. The one who instructs is to receive pay, Paul contends, in all good things. Paul argued in 1 Corinthians 9 strongly for paying the preacher, though he himself for special reasons refused to accept pay when in Corinth. Thus early do we find paid teachers or preachers in the churches. Those who were instructed came to be called " catechumens " from this verb. Today men talk a deal about " religious education," as if it were a new idea. It is only new in that some omit distinctive Christianity from " religious " or include the teachings of pagan religions as well. The early disciples saw the need of careful instruction in the elements of the Christian doctrines (Heb. 5: 12–6: 3).

The translation " communicate " for *koinōneō* is not felicitous. Lightfoot suggests " impart to " which is better. It means to be a partner with one, to share with one. Paul uses it for contributing to the necessities of the saints (Rom. 12: 13), and (Rom. 15: 27) argues that Gentile Christians are debtors to the Jewish Christians: " For if the Gentiles have been made partakers (*ekoinōnēsan*) of their spiritual things, they owe it to them also to minister unto them in carnal things." Hence Paul is taking the collection from the Gentile

Christians to the poor saints in Jerusalem. Precisely so
he here argues that the one taught share with his teacher
"in all good things," in all temporal mercies. "For if
we sowed for you the spiritual things, is it a great thing
if we reap your carnal things?" (1 Cor. 9: 11). This
is the spiritual commerce or exchange' for which a plea
is made here.

"Be not deceived: God is not mocked." Hear Lightfoot's paraphrase again: "What? You hold back?
Nay, do not deceive yourselves. Your niggardliness will
find you out. You cannot cheat God by your fair professions. You cannot mock him." If you do mock
(turn up the nose at, *muktērizō*) God, it is a dangerous
business as well as useless. Your outward profession of
God can be neutralized "by an indirect expression of
contempt" (Lightfoot) in your actual conduct in the
treatment of your ministers as well as in other failures
in generosity. This is "an evasion of his laws which
men think to accomplish, but, in fact, cannot" (Burton).
God has the last word when one is flippant toward him.
Pay the preacher with "good things" (money, food,
house, clothing), not just with compliments and kind
words. The old way of "pounding" the pastor comes
quite close to Paul's idea here.

Paul appeals to the well-known law of the harvest in
justification of what he has said about mocking God
by stinginess toward the preacher. "For whatsoever a
man soweth, that shall he also reap." This is one of
the commonest of proverbs and Paul already has it in
2 Corinthians 9: 6. The Galatians had been asked to
contribute to that same collection (1 Cor. 16: 1). Jesus
makes the same point in Matthew 7: 16-18. Men do not
gather grapes from thorns nor figs from thistles. The
Master has two parables along the same line, the parable
of the sower (Mark 4: 3-25) and the seed growing of
itself (Mark 4: 26-29). There are many elements that
go to the making of the harvest. Paul has already men-

tioned the kind of seed in verse 7, and now in verse 8
he discusses the kind of soil used in moral husbandry
(Lightfoot). The good tree is determined by the kind
of fruit, Jesus says (Matt. 7: 17f.). Rotten fruit is
proof of a rotten tree. The flesh produces rottenness
and corruption as Paul emphasizes in 1 Corinthians
15: 42. Life eternal will not grow upon a sensual life.
One who sows wild oats will reap an abundant harvest
beyond a doubt, but it will not be wheat. Surely this
wholesome lesson is greatly needed to-day when Freud
has damaged a generation of young people with his sex
complexes and psychoanalytic licenses. A life of ani-
malistic indulgence cannot result in spiritual strength.
Nature is a stern mistress and exacts punishment for the
violation of her laws. The spell of alcoholism can be
broken by the power of the Spirit of God in giving one
a new heart, but the drunkard is not a candidate for the
kingdom of God.

7. *Perseverance in Doing Good.*

" And let us not be weary in well doing." The verb
here translated " be weary in " (*enkakeō*) means literally
to be evil in, to behave badly in, to give in to evil.
Jesus uses it about praying with perseverance (Luke
18: 1). Paul has it in 2 Thessalonians 3: 13 in the
precise sense as here: " Be not weary in well-doing."
Here he says: " Let us not give in to evil while doing
the beautiful deed " (*to kalon*). In verse 10 he repeats
it thus: " Let us keep on doing the good deed " (*to
agathon*). Both ideas are thus brought in for " the
beautiful " and " the good." There is beauty in duty,
if we can only see it. Paul thus broadens the conception of our obligation to others to include all social
relations.

The final harvest is certain and it will be abundant
" if we faint not." Husbandmen are often overcome
with heat and fatigue as one may notice in the harvest

fields. The fainting (*ekluomenoi,* exhaustion, over re-
laxation, giving out) is a result of the growing weary
(*enkakeō,* giving in to evil), " the prostration of the
powers following on the submission of the will " (Lightfoot). There is but one thing to do, therefore " As we
have opportunity, let us keep on working (*ergazōmetha,*
present subjunctive) the good thing toward all men, and
especially toward the family of the faith." Paul clearly
recognizes a peculiar demand of believers in Christ on
one another because they are all members of God's
family. In Ephesians 2: 19 he describes Gentile Christians as no longer strangers, but " fellow-citizens with
the saints, and of the household of God " (very word,
oikeioi used here). Paul recognizes the special appeal
of the family of God as all Christians should.

It is worth asking why many people consider religious
service and worship dull and uninteresting, even tedious.
Some sermons, alas, are so, but that should not be. The
joy of doing the will of God should brighten any heart.
And then there is the added joy in the face and heart
of those who are benefited by a kindly deed that is
reward enough for keeping on doing the noble and
beautiful things as the opportunity comes for such
service. In Peter's sermon to Cornelius and his family
he described Jesus as one " who went about doing good
and healing all those who were overcome by the devil "
(Acts 10: 38). That is the perfect example for us all
in bearing one another's burdens.

VIII

YOUR PICTURE OF CHRIST

(A SERMON TO PREACHERS)

"The light of the knowledge of the glory of God in the face of Christ."—2 CORINTHIANS 4: 6.

THERE are many pictures of Christ by gifted artists through the centuries. Each gives the artist's own conception coloured by tradition. Most of them present a long-haired sentimental Christ of medieval Roman Catholicism, not the robust masterful Son of God and Son of man according to the Gospels. Fortunately there is no authentic portrait of Jesus, else it would have been worshipped as the images of him are to-day by many millions. As it is, there is in the church of St. Sylvester in Rome an alleged handkerchief portrait of Christ with a supposedly miraculous origin. The story is that Abgar, one of the kings of Edessa, wrote to Jesus, inviting him to come and heal him of his disease. Eusebius gives the correspondence with the reply of Jesus, both clearly fabrications. Moses of Chorene adds the story that Ananias, the messenger of Abgar, tried to paint a portrait of Jesus, but was so overcome by the splendour of Christ that he was compelled to quit. Then Jesus washed his face and wiped it with a towel and gave it to Ananias who took it, with the picture imprinted on it, to Abgar. It is all pure legend. We can be glad that no one did or can paint the picture of Christ. Hoffmann's " The Boy Jesus in the Temple " is to me the most satisfying of the many

83

attempts. But no artist has given us the strong masterful Christ, who wrought righteousness, fought the ecclesiastics of his day and the devil, died on the Cross for our sins, rose again triumphant over death, and will come again to judge the earth.

In simple truth each of us has to form his own picture of Christ in his heart. We must see him with the eyes of the heart illuminated (Eph. 1: 18) by the Holy Spirit, the Spirit of truth, who glorifies Christ and takes of the things of Christ and proclaims them unto us (John 16: 14) if we have ears to hear and eyes to see. David Smith has a delightful brochure, *The Face of Christ*, which undertakes to tell what he sees in the face of Christ. Men disagreed about Christ while he was upon earth and they disagree to-day. There were blind guides then, as there are now, who even charged that Jesus was in league with Beelzebub. It was the religious leaders (the Pharisees) who made that charge. In these verses (2 Cor. 4: 1–6) we have Paul's picture of Christ, drawn with his skilful touch. Do you agree with Paul? Do you see in the Face of Christ what Paul saw? Undoubtedly Paul refers to his own experience on the way to Damascus. That was both an inward and an objective experience. Paul then saw the Lord Jesus, risen from the dead, and he saw God in Christ. That Face of Christ remained with Paul always and moulded his whole life. How have you learned Christ, " as the truth is in Jesus " (Eph. 4: 20)? Is he just the greatest of men? Is he a deluded enthusiast? Is he the Son of God, the Son of man, the Saviour from sin, the mystery of God? Paul probably did not see Jesus in the flesh during his ministry, but he came to be the greatest interpreter of Christ to men. Paul met Jesus face to face and took him as his Master and Lord. If you see in the Face of Christ what Paul saw, several things follow which he here makes plain. And Jesus cares what we think of him.

1. *You Will Not Then Give in to Evil.*

Paul has in mind the ministry of the new covenant in Christ so clearly shown in the preceding chapter to be superior to that of the old covenant under Moses. He has in mind the continuous contact with Christ pictured in 3: 18, " beholding the glory of the Lord " Jesus and so " reflecting " that glory also as a blessed and illuminating radiance. This glorious ministry we all have as a precious " treasure in earthen vessels " (4: 7), a jewel in pieces of pottery " that the exceeding greatness of the power may be of God, and not from ourselves." So Paul " obtained mercy " (4: 1) in Christ's counting him worthy, " appointing me to his service " (1 Tim. 1: 12), me of all men in the world, considering what I was doing. The memory of this mercy and privilege stirs Paul here as always when he recalls it. It was Jesus who honoured Paul, not Paul who honoured Jesus.

Looking into the Face of Christ, says Paul, we do not give in to evil, we faint not, the same verb used in Galatians 6: 9 and again in 2 Corinthians 4: 16. The Face of Christ means to Paul courage (2 Tim. 1: 7). And the minister of Christ needs courage for Satan will not leave him alone. The devil did not spare Jesus himself, but returned repeatedly after his first defeat. He won Judas, tempted the rest of the group of the Twelve Apostles, and made Peter stumble into denial of his Lord. But Peter was rescued by the look and the special prayer of Jesus for him. Every disciple of Jesus has evil forced upon his notice, for we live in a world of sin and it is a constant fight to be in it and yet not of it. What do you say to the subtle allurements of Satan for a moment's lapse into the pleasures of sin? As for myself, says Paul (using the literary plural " we," but meaning himself, though speaking ideally for all of us), " I renounced the hidden things of shame " when they were presented to me. I did it once, do it now,

and will do it each time that Satan makes his offer.
Paul uses a word that means " to speak off from one."
I bade Satan begone as Jesus did to the devil on the
Mount of Temptation (Matt. 4: 10), and even when he
used Peter as his mouthpiece (Mark 8: 33). To parley
with Satan is to invite disaster. It is a pity for a
servant of Christ to have to know the hidden things of
shame at all, though sometimes it is inevitable. A
worker in the slums sees all kinds of evil and sometimes,
alas, vice allures and catches in its embrace the one who
condemns till he even condones and justifies and finally
enjoys it. Slumming parties by Christians are no longer
fashionable. They were always perilous. Jesus in the
temple ordered the grafters and profiteers out from the
desecration of the holy place. The new age in which
we live has flooded us all with a surfeit of sex stuff in
the name of scientific research and artistic realism. We
get an overdose of it in the daily newspapers, the magazines, the novels, besides the pornographic journals at
the news-stands too obscene to pass through the mails.
The Christian must regard all such hidden things of
shame as taboo for him. They besmear all who handle
them. The devil has almost captured the movies with
their pictures of immorality and of crime, training a
generation of criminals. He is fighting hard for the
radio in order to prove his lordship over the life of the
average man. Only the Lord can turn the light on the
hidden things of darkness (1 Cor. 4: 5) and when he
does the bats and the bugs that love the dark scamper
away. In *Pilgrim's Progress* Bunyan pictures the man
with the muckrake so enamoured of the nastiness that
he does not see the angel hovering above him. There
are nasty things in life, but we do not have to hold them
up to our noses till we enjoy the smell.

Paul adds about his own life that he does not walk in
craftiness. He had been accused in Corinth of being
a crafty man who would do anything to carry his point

(2 Cor. 12: 16), but that is flatly untrue. The end does not justify the means. The minister is not an unscrupulous lobbyist ready to offer or receive a bribe in order to win. Besides, says Paul, in preaching I do not handle the word of God deceitfully. The word comes from a word for bait (*dolos*) used to catch suckers. It was also used for adulterating gold or food. In 2: 17 Paul charged the Judaizers with " corrupting the word of God " as hucksters do by putting the best fruit on top of the basket. Paul vehemently resents the insinuations of his enemies in Corinth that he employed fallacious arguments in his interpretation of the Old Testament while he championed the freedom of grace as opposed to the bondage of the ceremonial law. Courage, therefore; and look again at the Face of Christ. There are legions of angels at his command. They that be with us are more and mightier than the enemies of Christ.

2. *You Will then Appeal to the Consciences of Men*

" But by the manifestation of the truth commending ourselves to every man's conscience in the sight of God," literally, " to every conscience of men," that is " to every kind of conscience, confident that they will *all* admit the justice of his claim " (Plummer). Every man has a conscience, that delicate instrument, planted in us all by God, " accusing or else excusing " (Rom. 2: 15). The conscience is not always right, because of deficient information, as was true of Paul when he was persecuting the disciples (Acts 23: 1). Some are past feeling from so much sinning (Eph. 4: 19). Some are branded in their consciences as with a hot iron (1 Tim. 4: 2); that is, they carry with them the perpetual consciousness of sin. And yet the word may mean " seared as with a hot iron " so that the conscience no longer plays its part. It is to the conscience that the preacher must appeal if he wishes results. For this purpose the Holy Spirit, " the Spirit of truth," is promised to us who " will convict the world in respect of sin, and of righteousness, and of judgment" (John 16: 8). That sort of preaching is what the world needs to-day. Passion, prejudice, reason are not safe guides. The conscience without the Holy Spirit is not infallible. How is the preacher to appeal to the consciences of men? There is no other effective way "but by the manifestation of the truth." "This is probably the simplest and most complete directory for the preaching of the Gospel. The preacher is to make the truth manifest" (James Denney). This is done by proclaiming the truth in Christ and by being a living epistle known and read of all men (2 Cor. 3: 1–6). Such "preaching of the truth of the gospel" (Col. 1: 5) calls for "no letters of recommendation, no wily arts, no crying of peace when there is no peace" (Plummer). The preacher's message and life are in the sight of God, not merely before men. The eye of God is upon every minister and every follower of Christ. There is no escape from the eye of the Searcher of souls with whom we have to do (Heb. 4: 13).

But even when the preacher's message is true and clear, and his life is clean, some are blinded so that they do not see. The gospel may be "veiled in them that perish: in whom the god of this world hath blinded the eyes of the unbelieving." It is true with some who hear Jesus that "seeing they see not, and hearing they hear not, neither do they understand" (Matt. 13: 13). There are blind guides to-day who fall into the pit with their followers (Matt. 15: 14). The veil is due to the blindness of men, not to the obscurity of the gospel of Christ. Even when Moses is read, it still lies upon many hearts (2 Cor. 3: 15). Satan claimed to Jesus to have power over the wicked world (Matt. 4: 8f.) and Jesus described him as the prince of this world (John 12: 31; 14: 30). It is for this reason that the *Zeitgeist*, the spirit of the time, is so largely hostile to Christ. The

terrible fact is that the whole world lies in sin (1 John
5: 19). Blinded by sin and led by blind guides men are
not able to see.

The very intellects (minds) of these men are darkened
" that the light of the gospel of the glory of Christ, who
is the image of God, should not dawn upon them." The
word dawn (*augē, augazō*) is the same root as the Ger-
man *Auge* (eye). The word for " light " is strictly " illumination " or brilliant radiance. The glory of Christ,
already pictured in 3: 18, bright enough to dazzle the
average eye, is not even perceived by those blinded by
Satan and in the grip of sin. They cannot even see the
Image of God in Christ. To Paul it was incredible that
men should not see the dazzling, overwhelming illumination in Jesus Christ. How blind are those who will not
see.

3. *You Will Preach Jesus, Not Self.*

" For we preach not ourselves, but Christ Jesus as
Lord." That may seem obvious enough, but it is by no
means universal. Some men do push themselves to the
fore even in preaching Christ so that it is difficult for
men to see the Lord Jesus. No more disgusting subject
for a sermon can be imagined than the preacher himself.
One day at dinner a little boy asked why the preacher
that day said " I " so much. The child had noticed it
and his father had difficulty in giving an answer that
protected the minister of the morning. Paul had been
accused of self-conceit (2 Cor. 3: 1) and of walking according to the flesh (2 Cor. 10: 2) because he commended
himself as an example for imitation by the Corinthians
(1 Cor. 4: 16; 7: 7; 11: 1). Christ and him crucified
(1 Cor. 2: 3) had been Paul's sole theme since he began
to preach. It will be so to the end with him as he exhorts
Timothy to remember Jesus Christ risen from the dead
(2 Tim. 2: 8). Paul preached not just the character of
Christ, matchless as that is; not just the heroic death

of Christ, true as that is; but the sacrificial and atoning death and resurrection of Christ and his glory on high. But for the resurrection " there would never have been such a thing as the Christian religion. We have a living Lord in whom all the redemptive virtue of a sinless life and death is treasured up, and who is able to save to the uttermost all that trust Him " (James Denney).

"And ourselves as your servants for Jesus' sake." That is the only proper place for the preacher, the " slave " of Christ and of Christ's followers. Paul is proud of being Christ's slave and because of that dignity offers himself to others. He is " yours to serve," and always " for Jesus' sake," *propter Jesum*. " It is not in order to curry favour with the Corinthians, or to flatter their conceit, that he counts himself as their *doulos* " (Plummer). It is all for the sake of Jesus Christ who emptied himself of his state of glory and took on himself the position of a slave (Phil. 2: 7) that Paul calls himself the " slave " of the Corinthians. When tempted to conceit, look at Jesus and see the tender love in his face. That will be enough. Preach Christ as Lord and live for him as Lord and look to him as Lord.

4. *And You Will Let the Light of God's Glory Shine Through You for Others.*

" Seeing it is God, that said, light shall shine out of darkness, who shined in our hearts, to give the light of the knowledge of the glory of God in the face of Jesus Christ." Paul makes a paraphrase of Genesis 1: 3 when God said: " Let there be light: and there was light." Those majestic words express simply God's power and glory. This verse gives Paul's reason why we must preach Christ, not ourselves. God did shine in our hearts and not merely in the creative act of giving light to the world. God is the Light and the Life of men (John 1: 4; 1 John 1: 5) and Christ as God's Son is also the Light of the world (John 8: 12). No doubt Paul has in mind the great experience when on the road to Damascus a light more brilliant than the noonday sun shone around him, a light that blinded his natural eyes, but he saw Jesus and that light has guided him since without failing. " In that face which flashed upon him by Damascus twenty years before, he had seen, and always saw, all that man could see of the invisible God " (James Denney).

The purpose of this shining of God in our hearts is " for the illumination (*phōtismon* again as in verse 4) of the knowledge of the glory of God in the face of Jesus Christ." Christ sent Paul to the Gentiles " to open their eyes, that they may turn from darkness to light, and from the power of Satan unto God " (Acts 26: 18). This illuminating power of the knowledge of the glory of God was given to Paul and to all followers of Christ who keep in touch with Christ so as to reflect his light and be like a city set on a hill (Matt. 5: 15). The purpose of the lamp is to shine, to give light. " Even so, let your light shine before men; that they may see your good works, and glorify your Father who is in heaven " (Matt. 5: 16).

Paul saw the glory of God in the face of Jesus Christ. What do you see in the face of Christ? " Many persons had looked on the face of Jesus while in the flesh who did not understand him. There was beyond doubt a wondrous fascination in the face of Jesus that no artist has succeeded in putting on canvas. The pictures of Christ are either too effeminate or too crude. No face has ever so haunted and baffled the greatest artists. This face was really human, but free from the taint of sin and disease. No spectres of the past looked through those eyes. No shadows of forbidden secrets flitted past. Pity, unutterable compassion looked out of the depths of purity and unsullied strength. Untarnished truth looked out on a world of lies. The noblest impulses of man met the shock of hate and envy. The clear light of heaven's love gazed lovingly at the suffering and the sinning. Those eyes could flash with terrific power upon hypocrites who used the livery of heaven to serve the devil in. Before his wrath men slunk away like cowed beasts, guilty and condemned. But the penitent and the contrite saw a new hope as they looked in the face of Jesus. There were some who could never forget the thrill of joy which came to their hearts as they gazed into his face. At moments they could be amazed at the struggling emotions in his countenance. There were three who beheld his majestic glory on the mount. But not all men could see all this in the face of Jesus. The rabbis were angered to desperation as they saw that calm and powerful face. Its very innocence enraged them. But Paul was a man gifted above his fellows. When once he did see Jesus Christ, he was in a position to see more than less gifted spirits. His soul was keyed to the highest tension as he looked into the face of Jesus. In his after study of that face he had the skill of a supreme artist. He never ceased looking."[1]

If men are to see in us the light of the knowledge of the glory of God, we must see that glory first ourselves (2 Cor. 3: 18), and see it here and now, and see it increasingly. Now it is dimly as in a mirror, save in rare and radiant experiences, but some day we shall see Christ face to face (1 Cor. 13: 12). Then we shall see him as he is in all the fulness of his majesty and glory (1 John 3: 2) and, more wonderful still, we shall be in some true sense like him, at last conformed to the Image of God's Son (Rom. 8: 29). Meanwhile we can glorify Christ here and now by so living with him that men may see some of Christ in us and take knowledge of us that we have been with Jesus.

[1] *The Glory of the Ministry*, pp. 87–9. A. T. Robertson. Revell.

IX

BUYING UP THE OPPORTUNITY

"Redeeming the time."—COLOSSIANS 4: 5; EPHESIANS 5: 16.

THE compound verb (*exagorazō*) here used in both Colossians and Ephesians means to go into the market (*agora*) and buy out (*ex*) of it what one needs. Paul has it also in Galatians 3: 13 of the redemptive work of Christ who "redeemed us from the curse of the law, having become a curse for us;" and again in Galatians 4: 5 "that he might redeem them that were under the law." Chrysostom explains it as meaning to buy off like a man who buys his life from a bandit who is about to kill him. So Bengel takes it as buying off from evil men and Calvin from the devil. In Daniel 2: 8 the very phrase employed here has the idea of gaining time. The figure here in Colossians and Ephesians is clearly that of one going into the open market and buying up for himself (middle voice) something of value, that is, the chance or opportunity of doing service for Christ.

1. Time Is Our Great Common Asset.

Time is the stuff out of which life is spun. It is a lesson that some never learn. As a matter of fact, now is the only time that we really possess. The past has gone by forever. The future is uncertain as to what it will bring. Now is the accepted time for coming to Christ, now is the day of salvation as Paul so powerfully argues (2 Cor. 6: 2) and now is the chance for service. The word used here for time is *kairos* which means opportunity, not time in general (*chronos*). It is the present opportunity, " the now time " (Rom. 8: 18), when the great decisions of life are made. The Spanish have a word, *mañana* to-morrow, which is a proverb for shiftless drifting and indecision. A nickname was once given to one of the French princes " Mr. Ten Minutes Late," that tells its own story of failure and defeat. The present time is the only universal possession. We do not all have health or wealth or power but we all do have the present moment of opportunity. The only certain thing about opportunity is that it is fleeting. John A. Broadus was fond of saying that opportunity is like a fleet horse that pauses restlessly by your side for a moment. Mount him and on you go; but hesitate, and he is gone. You can soon and for long hear the clattering of his feet as they echo down the corridor of time. Wasting time is throwing away the warp and woof of life itself. One may fling away his youth in dissipation and revelry. One may gamble away the prime of his life in idleness. One may dry up in old age and have nothing but bitter memories of wasted years with " nothing but leaves for garnered sheaves " that might have been the fruitage of time well spent. Time is long, but opportunity, our time, is fleeting.

2. *Buying Up Time a Mark of Wisdom.*

In the market place the best bargains are secured by those who come first and who are willing to pay the price. In turning time into opportunity there is competition. There are companions for idlers and loafers, but we have competitors in the wise use of time. Paul means for us to " seize the opportunity " while we have it, " making your market to the full from the opportunity of this life " (W. M. Ramsay), " letting no opportunity slip you of saying and doing what may further the cause of God " (Lightfoot). There is need of practical wisdom such as Christ urged upon the Twelve when he sent them forth with instructions to be wise as serpents and yet harmless as doves (Matt. 10: 1). "Look therefore carefully how ye walk, not as unwise, but as wise" (Eph. 5: 15). The "carefully" or "accurately" in the correct text goes with "look," not with "walk" as the Authorized Version has it. In walking upon ice the essential thing is to look carefully before you place your feet. The walking must also be done accurately, but the looking comes before the leaping or stepping. "Let him that thinketh he standeth take heed lest he fall" (1 Cor. 10: 12). Presumption explains many a fall, even from a great height. Buying up the opportunity does not mean rashness. In these days one must look quickly in every direction before crossing the street and then go at once across. The wise man learns how to use his time, to work when he works, to rest when he rests, to sleep when he sleeps. The wise use of time is to do it before it is too late. The author of the Epistle to the Hebrews exhorts us to come with boldness to the throne of grace "that we may obtain mercy and find grace to help in time of need" (4: 16). "Well-timed help," the phrase means, help in the nick of time, help while there is opportunity to save. Many a man has drowned because help came after he had gone down the last time. Many a soul has missed heaven by putting off a decision for Christ till the convenient season that never came. The five foolish virgins finally got their oil for their lamps, but they waited too long to get it. While they went away to buy, the bridegroom came and the door was shut. In vain they begged: "Lord, Lord, open to us." The Lord answered without opening the door: "Verily I say unto you, I know you not" (Matt. 25: 11).

3. *And in Particular Is Such Wisdom Called For Toward Non-Christians.*

"Walk in wisdom toward them that are without, redeeming the time" (Col. 4: 5). Those outside the fold of Christ watch with keen eyes the walk of those who claim to be Christians. They have a right to eye us keenly to see if we are sincere or merely professional followers of Christ, in short, hypocrites. The Jews called the heathen "those without." Paul reminds the Ephesians "that ye were at that time separate from Christ, alienated from the commonwealth of Israel, and strangers from the covenants of the promise, having no hope and without God in the world" (Eph. 2: 12). In writing to the Thessalonians (1 Thess. 4: 12) Paul reminds them of his former charge, "that ye may walk becomingly toward them that are without." The eyes of the world are upon us. We have no right to complain and surely wish to be honest and open in all our dealings with men. Peter carries the same truth when he says: "For so is the will of God, that by well-doing ye should put to silence the ignorance of foolish men: as free, and not using your freedom for a cloak of wickedness, but as bondservants of God" (1 Pet. 2: 15f.). Gipsy Smith in his new book, *The Beauty of Jesus*, tells of speaking once to an elevator man and saying: "I hope you love Jesus." The man thanked him warmly and said that was the first time in twenty-five years that anybody had spoken to him about his soul. A similar story is told of Minister Wu. When his distinguished term of service was ended and he was about to return to China, a friend somewhat hesitatingly asked if he would like to go to church with him on his last Sunday. He assented heartily, saying, "I made up my mind when I came over that if I were asked to go into a Christian church I would gladly go. This is the first time I have been asked." Does Paul not mean by wisdom toward those without that we buy up the opportunity before it is gone? That we make this present moment, untoward as it may seem, the day of salvation? There are always difficulties in the way, obstacles, hindrances, excuses, that must be brushed aside. Napoleon said there shall be no Alps and went on over them into Italy. Faith like a grain of mustard seed, said Jesus, will remove the sycamine tree, this mountain, this anything that stands in the path of privilege and of duty. Many a soul has heard God's call over the radio and answered it then and there. Decide now for Christ. There are thousands of unsaved persons all around us. The fields are white for the harvest. The labourers are few. Still we dally and parley and postpone seeking to win to Christ those right at our doors. We are not redeeming the time. We are not then walking wisely toward those without the kingdom of God.

4. Such Wisdom in the Use of Opportunity Is Urgent When the Days Are Evil.

"Redeeming the time, because the days are evil" (Eph. 5: 16). This is Paul's reason for buying up time and seizing the opportunity. The days are evil, hard times have come, the depression hangs on. "There is a bad harvest; the food supply is short, you must haste to the market and buy up for yourselves" (Walter Lock). In the jail in Philippi we see Paul buying up the opportunity to preach Christ to the frightened jailor (Acts 16: 28–33). He lost no time, but then and there in the midst of the excitement told the way of life to the jailor and won him to Christ with all his house. Dr. Lock thinks that Paul here may recall the words in Sirach 4: 20: "Observe the opportunity and beware of evil." The evil days are not just hard times which we all know so well, but morally evil days, "this present evil age" (Gal. 1: 4). "The moments for sowing on receptive soil in such evil days being few, seize them when they offer themselves" (Abbott). It is a temptation to us all to blame the times for our own failure. The truth may be just the opposite. Bad times offer unusual opportunities for Christians to get a hearing for Christ if we have the skill to use them. John A. Broadus

wrote on the fly-leaf of his New Testament at this place
some suggestive comments concerning evil times: (a)
Evil times leave many opportunities unimproved. So
many excuse themselves from service then. (b) Evil
times bring many opportunities of their own that otherwise we should not have. (c) Do not dream what you
might do at some other time, but do what you can do
now. Surely there is consummate wisdom in these re-
marks and they properly interpret Paul's message here.
When trouble of any kind comes (like poverty, sickness,
disgrace, death), some will listen then who will not hear
us at other times. In the days of prosperity they wear
an attitude of pride or even of scorn, but in the days
of adversity the heart is humbled before God and men.
This is an open door, if we have walked wisely so that
our words will be accepted at their face value.

5. *Conversation Offers Special Opportunity for Such
     Wisdom.*

" Let your speech be always with grace, seasoned with
salt, that ye may know how ye ought to answer each
one " (Col. 4: 5). This is a special phase of " walking
in wisdom," proper behaviour toward those without. It
is not just sermons that Paul has in mind by the combination of grace and salt, though sermons certainly are
more effective if both elements are present. " Your
speech " includes conversation also. The ancient Greek
writers often spoke of the *charis logōn*, the charm of
words. In Psalm 45: 2 we have the beautiful expression: " Grace is poured upon thy lips." Pleasingness (or
grace) is the garb with which speech is to be invested
(Ellicott). But more than mere pleasantness is required
for the spiritual palate. Sweetness alone palls upon the
taste. Talk must be " seasoned with salt " to be palat-
able and to be wholesome. Salt is a preservative. Jesus
termed Christians " The salt of the earth " (Matt. 5:
13). But salt itself has no value when it has lost its

savour. " It is thenceforth good for nothing but to be
cast out and to be trodden under foot of men." A salt-
less Christian is like a sucked orange with all the pith
and flavour gone. Jesus even says that such salt is
hopeless and useless. The opposite of speech seasoned
with salt as a preservative is " rotten speech " (logos
sapros, Eph. 4: 29) which does come out of the mouth
and from the pen of some people, like the "filthiness,"
" foolish talking," " jesting," so strongly condemned by
Paul (Eph. 5: 4). " Let no corrupt speech proceed out
of your mouth, but such as is good for edifying as the
need may be, that it may give grace to them that hear "
(Eph. 4: 29). Does our speech, seasoned with salt, give
grace to those that hear?

But salt was used also to give flavour to the palate
and to keep food from being insipid (mōros, not sapros
rotten). Words without salt are like bread without salt
(Job 6: 6), tasteless. This is the main idea here. Salt
is here a metaphor for wit, for sense. It was common
for heathen writers (Cicero, for instance) to insist that
discourse should be seasoned with salt. Both Plutarch
and Dio Chrysostom urge also the importance of the
connection between grace (charis) and wit (hals).
Their idea of " salt " in talk is wit, which easily degen-
erates into vulgarity. But Attic salt was the wit that
gives speech point and pertinency and keeps it from being dull. There is no reason in the world why pious
people should be humdrum and prosaic in their talk,
nor why sermons should be a bore. The ideal is what
Paul commends, the union of charm and salt, grace and
gumption. There is pungent wit in the table talk of
Jesus. He praises the Syro-Phœnician woman for the
brightness and wit of her repartee, " For this thy saying,
go thy way " (Mark 7: 29). There is the crack of a
whip in the words of Jesus in the terrible woes to the
Pharisees in Matthew 23. There is sometimes malicious-
ness in words like the tares sown by the evil one (Matt.

13: 25). Then one needs the best powers of the intellect and the Spirit of God to be " able to quench all the fiery darts of the evil one " (Eph. 6: 16).

" That ye may know to answer each one." Our conversation must be opportune as to time and appropriate as to the person (Lightfoot). Paul himself tried to be all things to all men in a high and holy sense (1 Cor. 9: 22), not for mere flattery or for glory from his hearers (1 Thess. 1: 5f.). Answering questions from so many kinds of people with all sorts of problems (real and imaginary) is an art that taxes the skill of the greatest teachers. " Each individual, whether putting his questions from malice or ignorance, sincerity or insincerity, was separately to receive the appropriate answer to his inquiry " (Ellicott). If one wishes to follow Paul's career for illustrations as to how he himself answered various individuals, one will find it edifying and profitable. See Paul before Elymas Barjesus at Paphos, the Judaizers at Antioch and Jerusalem, the jailor at Philippi, the Epicureans and Stoics in Athens, the high priest Ananias in Jerusalem, Felix and Festus in Cæsarea, the Jews in Rome. So then " sanctify in your hearts Christ as Lord: being ready always to give answer to every man that asketh you a reason concerning the hope that is in you, yet with meekness and fear " (1 Pet. 3: 15). The Christian has no reason to be ashamed of his faith and hope anywhere, at any time, before any one (king or peasant). The one who holds converse with the King of Kings can lift his head up everywhere.

X

PAUL'S IDEALS FOR DEACONS

1 TIMOTHY 3: 8–13.

IT is probable, though not certain, that the origin of the office of deacon is seen in Acts (6: 1–6) as a result of the murmuring of the Hellenistic Jewish believers in the daily distribution of the funds for the poor. It was claimed that the widows among the Hellenists were overlooked in favour of the Aramæan widows "in the daily ministration" (*diakonia*). So the apostles selected seven Hellenistic brethren to attend to this business, saying: "It is not fit that we should forsake the word of God, and serve (*diakonein*) tables." The word "deacon" (*diakonos*) does not here occur, but the same root appears in the words for "ministration" and "serve." In Philippians 1: 1 we find "bishops and deacons" named as the officers of the church. So in writing to Timothy Paul discusses the qualifications of bishops or elders (both terms for the same office) and then of deacons, the same two classes of church officers seen in Philippians 1: 1.

The original meaning of *diakonos* is one who executes the commands of another, a servant, attendant, minister. Thayer gives the etymology of the word as *dia* (through, thorough), and *konis* (dust), "raising dust by hastening." So in the account of the marriage at Cana the word *diakonos* occurs for "waiters" and in the words of Jesus in Matthew 20: 26: "Whosoever shall be great among you shall be your minister." It is frequently employed for preachers like our "ministers" as in the case of Paul and other "ministers of God" and "ministers of the new

101

covenant." Even a magistrate may be termed "a minister of God" (Rom. 13: 4). Men can be "ministers" of Satan or of Christ (2 Cor. 11: 15, 23). But the technical sense of "deacon" in contrast to "bishops" or "elders" occurs only in Romans 16: 1; Philippians 1: 1; 1 Timothy 3: 8–13. Paul alone discusses the qualifications for this important office. "No definition of duties is given" (Lock), and Parry argues that the deacon is not a separate office from the elder or bishop, but only a variety of elder (a serving, not a governing, elder). But this view is not sustained by Paul's language here in 1 Timothy.

1. The Deacon's Demeanour.

"Deacons in like manner must be grave." In like manner with "the bishop" of verse 2. The same adjective (*semnas*) is repeated about women in verse 11 and about aged men in Titus 2: 2. It is an old word from *sebō* to revere, to worship, and always means an honourable, venerated character. Paul does not say that the deacon must be an aged man, but he should be, whether old or young, reverent in attitude and demeanour and respected for his noble qualities. He is not to be a light and flippant man, a kind of male flapper. To attempt to imitate Bunyan in giving names of qualities to individuals, he is not to be Deacon Giddy, not by any remote possibility. That would be to make the office a joke and a laughing-stock.

2. The Deacon's Conversation.

"Not double-tongued." Originally the word (*dilogos*) meant saying a thing twice. The sense of double-tongued or saying one thing to one person, another to another, as Paul here uses it, does not occur elsewhere. But there are other words made like it such as *dipsuchos* or double-minded (Jas. 1: 8), *diglōssos* (double-tongued, deceitful, a tale-bearer, Prov. 11: 13), *distomos* (two-mouthed, or two-edged, Heb. 4: 12), *diprosōpos* (two-faced, Testimony of the Twelve Patriarchs). Bunyan in *Pilgrim's Progress* speaks of " the parson of one parish, Mr. Two Tongues." James tells of the same mouth that utters blessing for God and cursing for men in God's likeness (Jas. 3: 9f.). The deacon, therefore, is not to be a tattler, a tale-bearer, a gossip, a meddler. When he does speak he must mean what he says and not speak with his tongue in his cheek. He must be able to hold his tongue on occasion and not be quick to answer. He must be able to think twice before he speaks at all. There must be discretion in his words and his word must be as good as his bond. Reliability, not volubility, is the true mark of the deacon's speech. He may be learned, bilingual or he may speak more than two languages, but his words must mean the same thing in any tongue. In a word, he must not be Deacon Babbler. His tongue must not be loose at both ends. The deacon ought to be able to pray in public and to bear witness to God's grace to him. In sooth, the members of the church should not be able to quote the deacon on opposite sides of the same question.

3. The Deacon's Habits.

" Not given to much wine." He must be temperate. The idiom here is a common one and literally means " not holding the mind on much wine." It is temperance certainly, and, if necessary, abstinence. In Palestine wine was usually drunk with two-thirds water. Paul does not here make total abstinence from the use of wine as a beverage necessary in the deacon, but he does require that he shall drink it sparingly, if he uses it at all. Temperance with some people has come to mean that you must drink some wine. That is a complete reversal of the point. The thing that Paul here requires is that no man who puts his mind on the bottle, who is a regular drinker, least of all a drunkard, shall be chosen as a deacon. In going from house to house a social glass might be offered the deacon. He must be on his guard. It is a reproach to any church to have as a deacon a man who gets drunk. It is a disgrace to him and to the cause of Christ. The deacon should not be a tippler. He should not be Deacon Toper. He should not be a dope-fiend, a glutton, a drunkard, or a gambler. The power of God can save the worst of men, but these are not the ones to elect as deacons. A habit is something that we have and that also has us. No man in the grip of an evil habit, vice, or sin is fit to be a deacon. No trace of immorality with women should besmirch his character or reputation. Deacons of unclean life will paralyze any church. No plea of personal liberty should be allowed for such vicious indulgences with wine, women, gambling, or crooked business habits, no matter what one's social connections may be. The bishop also was not to be one who stays by the wine (1 Tim. 3: 3).

4. *The Deacon's Use of Money.*

" Not greedy of filthy lucre." The preacher is not to be a lover of money (verse 3) and in Titus 1: 7 Paul uses this same adjective employed here about the deacon, " not greedy of filthy lucre." The word means " shameful gain " (*aischrokerdēs*), shameful if made by unclean or disgraceful methods as is sometimes true of " tainted money "; shameful use of money also if misappropriating or mishandling church funds. This latter point is particularly appropriate in the case of deacons since the office arose from complaints concerning the aid for the widows in Jerusalem. This caution thus pertains to the fundamental employment of deacons. Parry takes the phrase " not greedy of filthy lucre " to mean " making small gains in mean ways." The deacon must not be in the grip of the money-devil. He must not make money his god. He must not worship mammon even if he professes to worship God. Jesus says this double worship is impossible. He must be a man of business integrity and of known liberality and generosity in the use of his money, a tither at least. He must not be Deacon Skinflint. He must not be the slave of money, but make money his slave. Covetousness is a sin that no Christian should commit, let alone a deacon or a preacher. No money made by fraud should be in a deacon's hands. No money derived from shameful sources should be his. A man of business integrity alone should be a deacon.

5. *The Deacon's Spirituality.*

"Holding the mystery of the faith in a pure conscience." Paul wishes the deacon to be a man that is not merely orthodox in his beliefs, as he ought to be, but one who goes deeper into " the secret truths of the Christian faith," like " the mystery of godliness " in verse 16 which is manifested in Christ. This means that the deacon should be a man of some intelligence, not necessarily an educated man in the fullest sense, but a man of insight and balance, not a crotchety, fly-by-night believer. Many a plain man with little learning has a clear grasp of the Christ who is the mystery of God revealed to us. He is a man with " a true inward religion and a true inward morality " (Hort). A man must live the mystery of the faith if he is to hold it and keep it, and especially if he is to speak of it to others, as every deacon ought to be able to do. The first seven deacons were to be " men full of the Spirit and of wisdom " (Acts 6: 3). He is to be a spiritually-minded man, who holds the mystery of the faith " in a pure conscience," which is " the casket in which the jewel is to be kept " (Lock). He is not to be Deacon Hypocrite. His faith and his life must have the note of reality and sincerity. The deacon should be a man who, if he preaches, will make no one gasp with surprise. Stephen and Philip, two of the first deacons, became great preachers of Christ.

6. The Deacon's Experience.

"And let these also first be proved." The verb for proving here is a very common one, used for testing metals, as gold tested by fire (1 Pet. 1: 7). After the testing comes approval or disapproval. Paul is not here alluding to a formal examination of the deacon as to his doctrines and life. The proving or testing is done by the man's life previous to his selection as deacon. He should not be chosen for this high office without enough time to show what sort of a life the man is really living. Some think that the deacon is to have a period of probation after the election before he is formally set apart. But that is hardly what Paul has in mind. Just as the preacher is to have good testimony from all, in and out of the church, so the deacon should be chosen from among men with real experience of grace. It is always a pity to see a new convert made a deacon or set apart as a preacher at once upon conversion, particularly if he has led an openly evil life up till his conversion. A little time to prove one's metal is wise. It is true that Christ called Saul to preach at the time of his conversion, but even he, after beginning to preach in Damascus, spent three years in Arabia in readjusting his old views to the new and revolutionary point of view in Christ. The deacon must not be Deacon Greenhorn, but a man of wisdom, whether old or young in years.

7. The Deacon's Reputation.

"Then let them serve as deacons, if they be blameless." One may have a good character and a bad reputation, or one may have a good reputation and a bad character. The deacon should be above reproach in his reputation in the community if he is to have an influence for good. The word here (anegklētos) means one who cannot be called to account, unaccused, and is used in Titus of the bishop also. This is a high standard, most assuredly, for there are few men against whom no wag-

ging tongues hurl any charge at all. But, at any rate,
the deacon must see to it that such charges are untrue,
that they are false slanders in a word. The church
should not be embarrassed and put on the defensive by
the life of the deacon. He should not be Deacon Bad
Odour. This evil reputation should not smell to heaven.
Where there is much smoke there is apt to be some fire.
But church members should not pick flaws in the deacon's life when he is not guilty of wrong-doing. The
word here for serving as deacon (*diakoneō*) is the same
one that occurs in Acts 6: 2 about serving tables.

8. The Deacon's Domestic Life.

"Let deacons be husbands of one wife, ruling their
children and their own houses well." This does not mean
that the deacon must be a married man, but simply that
he must not be a polygamist. He must have only one
wife at a time, if a married man. This same require-
ment is made of the bishop in verses 2 and 4. There
and here also Paul can hardly mean that the bishop or
deacon must be a married man in view of his own
personal preference for celibacy. Polygamy still existed
among the Jews as in the case of the ten wives of Herod
the Great. Precisely this problem confronts missionaries
in heathen lands to-day. Clearly preachers and deacons
in such regions must not be polygamists. Christ's strict
views about divorce, endorsed by Paul, would forbid
remarriage after divorce except for the innocent party
in the case of fornication or adultery. Some of the early
Christian writers (Tertullian, Clement of Alexandria,
Origen) hold that Paul here forbids remarriage by the
elder or deacon in case his wife dies. But that is a
strained interpretation of Paul's language. As with the
bishop, so with the deacon, in the matter of the children.
He is to rule well his children, if he has any, and his
own household. The word for " rule " means to stand
in front of (*proistamai*). It occurs in 1 Thessalonians

(5: 12) for the leaders in the church and in Titus (3: 8) for those who take the lead in good works. Paul touches here the essential element in the position of the husband and father. He is the head of the family and cannot shirk his responsibility. Wife and children do not always follow the lead of a pious and consecrated husband and father, but it is his privilege and duty to take the lead in the way that points to God. He should not be Deacon Henpeck. People watch eagerly for slips and jars in the family life of preachers and deacons. But it remains true that the homes of devout Christians are the happiest in the whole country and produce the best citizens.

9. The Deacon's Reward.

" For they that have served well as deacons gain to themselves a good standing, and great boldness in the faith which is in Christ Jesus." The word for " standing " (*bathmon*) means steps in walking (2 Kings 20: 9), a step at the door (1 Sam. 5: 5), steps on the stairs, a platform, foothold or standing place (inscriptions). The word is used of promotions in the army and in the ecclesiastical writers for higher ministerial rank. Some take Paul here to mean that the deacon who serves well will be promoted to be a bishop. But that is not in harmony with the context. It is a good standing as a deacon that one wins, not the position of bishop (elder). Success as a deacon wins for one a noble place in the hearts of the people and encourages the deacon to great boldness in the faith. The examples of Stephen and Philip are clearly pertinent. They did take to preaching and Stephen became the first martyr for Christ, and Philip the first evangelist in the technical sense. But not all deacons can or should become bishops or elders, though one should have boldness enough to bear witness for Christ at any time, in private life and in public if need be. He should not be Deacon Weak Knees. He should

be ready at all times to respond to every call for Christ.
Thus he occupies a place of strategic importance, full
of honour and dignity.

10. Deaconesses.

"Women in like manner must be grave, not slanderers,
temperate, faithful in all things." This verse (11) comes
right in the midst of Paul's discussion of deacons and
makes it seem certain that he means here by "women"
either the "wives" of deacons or women as deaconesses.
Greek commentators mostly took it to be wives of deacons, though Chrysostom took it to mean deaconesses.
The items mentioned are not particularly those of a
wife, one may observe. There is the case of Phœbe who
is expressly called "a deaconess (*diakonos*) of the
church in Cenchrea" (Rom. 16: 1). Women did serve
as deaconesses in the early centuries. "Their duties in
later times are defined as instructing and attending at
the baptism of female catechumens, of looking after
them at the services and taking messages from the
bishops to them" (Lock). The word for "grave" is the
same as that applied to deacons in verse 8. The word
for "slanderers" (*diabolous*) is devils. Women as deaconesses must not be "she-devils." Paul makes the
same prohibition about aged women in Titus 2: 3.
"While men are more prone to be *dilogous*, double-
tongued, women are more prone than men to be slanderers" (White). They are to be "temperate" also as
the bishop is (verse 2). In a word, they are to be
"faithful in all things." As almoners, the women had
special temptations. These requirements do not exclude
reference to domestic duties, but they seem more pertinent to church duties (Ellicott). If the reference is to
women as deaconesses, she is not to be Mrs. Gossip. The
organized work in most modern churches gives women
even more power and effectiveness than the early deaconesses had.

XI

THE ONE-TALENT MAN

Matthew 25: 13–30

THIS parable is sometimes taken to be a variation of the Parable of the Pounds in Luke (19: 11–27), but that is not the case. " The lesson of the Pounds is, that men endowed with the same gifts may make a very different use of them and be very differently requited. The lesson of the Talents is, that men with different gifts may make an equally good (or bad) use of them, and be proportionately requited " (Plummer). Each supplements the other, but they are not identical. There is a similarity in some respects, but a popular preacher like Jesus would on different occasions use similar stories to illustrate his points. It should be noted here that the Parable of the Talents is to enforce the exhortation in verse 13: " Watch therefore, for ye know not the day 'nor the hour." The Parable of the Ten Virgins just before showed that those who watch for the second coming of Christ must be " wise " while this Parable of the Talents proves that they must be " faithful." The waiting may be long, but the Master will come in his own good time.

Two of those receiving talents make a hundred per cent. increase (five plus five, two plus two). They both receive the same praise (" good and faithful servant ") with a share in the joy of their lord and promotion to still higher service to be in charge of many things. But we are here concerned with the one-talent man who presents a problem in unused power. This is the gravest matter in church inefficiency. It concerns both ministers

and all other church members. The word here for talent does not apply only to money, but to all the gifts
and graces with which one is endowed. Our very words
" talent " and " talented " come from this parable. De-
velopments in the use of hydro-electric power have
shown what can be done with the unused natural re-
sources all about us. The neglect to use the powers
which we have is the chief cause of the slow progress in
the Christian life and the kingdom of God. Dr. Russell
H. Conwell had a famous lecture on " Acres of Dia-
monds," which lie all about us, under our very feet if we
only had eyes to see and mind to use what we have. Let
us study the One-Talent Man as pictured by Jesus.

1. *He Accepted His Responsibility for the One Talent.*

He took it from the hand of his Master with the distinct understanding that he would use it for the benefit
of his lord. As a matter of fact, a talent was not a
negligible sum. It was about a thousand dollars and
that is a great deal more money than many people have
at one time. In times of unemployment multitudes are
out of funds and some do not wish work. There are, to
be sure, persons with no moral responsibility like idiots
and the insane. But these can be left to one side. They
are not considered in this parable. They form a very
small percentage in the company of nominal Christians.
Very well, then. We admit that we possess moral responsibility. How many talents do we acknowledge or
admit? In the twelfth chapter of First Corinthians Paul
presents a varied list of the gifts of the Holy Spirit in
the church in Corinth. They differed greatly, but each
member was responsible for the gift or gifts that he
actually had, not for those possessed by others and not
by him. It is amazing how humble people sometimes
are when they are asked to do certain things for the
cause of Christ. They have a sudden attack of the in-
feriority complex and if a collection is going on feel

suddenly poor. But certainly we all will have to admit that we are entrusted with at least one talent by our Lord and Master who is now in the far country. He will come back and demand a reckoning from us for the one talent or more that we possess. Dr. Broadus used to say that one was a big per cent. on nothing. The addition of many zeros makes only zero. But one is a definite and positive start. Surely the do-nothing and give-nothing members of our churches do not admit that they are zeros in the kingdom of God. But we are ciphers unless we can make our talent multiply into two talents.

2. This Man Had All that He Was Able to Handle.

Each received " according to his several ability." This is the law of grace. Men are not born equal in capacity, though all should be born free and with equal privileges and opportunities. Even if all men could start with perfect equality, they would not long remain so as the Parable of the Pounds clearly shows. There is diversity of use, even when there is equality of opportunity. Paul makes all this perfectly plain: " But all these things the one and the same Spirit works, distributing to each one severally even as he wills " (1 Cor. 12: 11). Let each of us rejoice in the gift that God has given us with no jealous heart or eye toward those with other and perhaps nobler gifts. The thing is for each to use with gratitude to the full the gift bestowed on us by the Spirit (Rom. 12: 6). We forget that the gift of God, whether by inheritance or birth is no occasion for personal pride. " For who makes thee to differ? And what dost thou have that thou didst not receive? But if thou didst receive it, why dost thou glory as if thou hadst not received it? " (1 Cor. 4: 7). There is no ground for conceit in all this for any of us. On the other hand, no one should feel unduly depressed by the limitations of his environment or the smallness of his task. Jesus said: " He that is faithful in a very little is faithful also in much "

(Luke 16: 10). God shows the same care in the structure of the atom that he exhibits in the whirling of the stars, as Dr. Harris E. Kirk shows in *Atoms, Stars and God*. The personal equation is a factor in every problem that exerts a tremendous influence on the outcome. There are plenty of inequalities in our laws and in our living conditions that need to be remedied. But, when such social reforms are realities, the millennium will still not be on hand. Individual initiative differs and makes socialism unable to guarantee success or happiness to all. The problem for each of us is far simpler. It is for each one to use the gift that he has, to use it wisely, to use it to the full extent of one's capacity and environment. The amount of work turned out will vary greatly. A man once proposed a plan to raise ten million dollars a year for missions by each one of four million church members in his denomination giving five cents a Sunday. On paper the thing seems simple enough. Many a little does make a mickle in street-car fares, in soda water, chewing-gum, cosmetics. But getting everybody to give to missions is quite another story.

3. This Man Did Not Use What He Had.

" But he that received the one went away and digged in the earth, and hid his lord's money." He evidently got in a huff at the disparity in the gifts because he considered himself equal to either of the others. He was mad as a hornet and " went off and dug and hid," a graphic picture of his tearing rage and passion. As a matter of fact, it was not his money to hide anyhow. There is said to be an enormous amount of buried money in India. The long depression caused some of it to come into circulation. Misers are fond of hiding their money in secret places, some of which is never found. A miserly spinster in a Virginia city hid her money, not in a stocking, but between the bed-ticks, in the chinks of the walls, in all sorts of odd places, most of which was discovered after her death. It is tragic to think of the buried talents in the lives of Christians. Every church has hidden treasures in the members who have not been put to use, who have never been drawn out into active service. I have heard letters from churches to Baptist district Associations which say that the church is doing well, holding its own, holding it very tight, one may add. This man's jealousy blinded him to the law of promotion in business. That always comes to the man who does well the task that he has. So many people feel able to do better a job that they do not have, who are careless about the one they do possess. " Unto every one that hath shall be given, and he shall have abundance." Life grows and not to grow is to die.

4. *This Man Blamed Some One Else for His Own Failure.*

He came up last, but he had his tale ready. " And he also that had received the one talent came and said, Lord, I knew thee that thou art a hard man, reaping where thou didst not sow, and gathering where thou didst not scatter; and I was afraid, and went away and hid thy talent in the earth: lo, thou hast thine own." This is the lazy jealous scamp's excuse for his own conduct. His very words condemn him and prove him to be a " wicked and slothful servant " as his master called him. His own confession shows him to be unworthy of the trust committed to him. He was slow and incompetent and unworthy of more responsibility. " Thou oughtest therefore to have put my money to the bankers, and at my coming I should have received back mine own with interest." That was the very least that the utmost caution and prudence called for. Even if he did not know how to turn over money so as to make more money, there were men who made it their business. There are people who do not know how to keep money. It slips through their fingers like water. They are spendthrifts and extravagant squanderers. But this man was a hoarder, a " deacon skinflint " kind of man, a tight-wad, a deadweight. He accused his master of having a bad reputation and expressed fear of being blamed by him if anything happened to the master's old talent. So he hid it and now returns it safely with a load of anxiety gone: " Lo, thou hast thine own." This talent of thine, he means, has been a leaden burden upon my spirit. At any rate, he argues, he has not lost the talent, as he might have done. This is obscurantism and conservatism run into the ground and broken off. The farmer does not always reap a good harvest, but, if he never sowed any grain, he would never have any harvest. Banks do not always get back the money loaned out, but, if they never loaned any to anybody, they would never make any money. This man claimed personal knowledge of his master's " close-fistedness " and so was unwilling to take any risks with a man like that. He accused his lord of taking advantage of the toil of other men, of being a Shylock, an oppressor of those under him. So he is glad to be rid of this talent and to have the thing off of his mind. This is the pious pose of the good-for-nothing scoundrel. " He wickedly misjudged and slandered his master, and tried to make that an excuse for his slothful failure to do as he had been commanded. The master retorts that his own excuse establishes his guilt " (Broadus). In the master's reply he does not deny that he is " a hard money-making Jew " (Plummer), but even so that offers no excuse for the worthless slave. " The master smites him with his own weapon " (B. Weiss). He was too lazy to trade, to do business with the one talent so as to make more. Clement of Alexandria quotes a saying of Jesus, not in our Gospels: " Become wise bankers." That saying is at least like Jesus, whether genuine or not. It is an exceedingly dull man who cannot find plenty of good excuses for his own patent failures.

5. *This Man Lost the One Talent that He Had.*

" Take ye away, therefore, the talent from him, and give it unto him that hath the ten talents." He had proven himself unworthy. So the one-talent man became the no-talent man. He was an " unprofitable " servant and it was sheer waste of time and money to leave the talent with him longer. This is the law of nature. Atrophy overtakes organs in the body that are not used. In the Mammoth Cave in Kentucky the fish in Echo River have eye sockets, but no eyes. Living in continual darkness has caused the eyes to disappear because they were not able to function. This law applies to the non-use of the mind as well as of the body. Charles Darwin is said to have confessed toward the close of his life that he had lost the faculty of appreciating the spiritual side of life. That is a terrible price to pay for even the great discoveries in physical science. There is great peril in unemployment in times of depression. Hobos or tramps have lost the power of steady application. They have become like wandering stars and are unable to focus their powers upon a given task. " But from him that hath not, even that which he hath shall be taken away." That seems hard, but it is just. It is the law of life and of God. It is the survival of the fittest in the highest and truest sense. The word rendered " hath " here is in the present tense and means to keep on having, to keep on gaining. " If no attempt is made to render effective service, it will be useless to plead that the sphere was very narrow and very humble, or that we did nothing for fear of making mistakes. To do nothing is often the greatest mistake of all the possibilities " (Plummer).

6. *This Man Lost His Own Soul.*

" And cast ye out the unprofitable servant into the outer darkness: there shall be the weeping and the gnashing of teeth." The two others were invited to enter the joy of their lord within the house. This useless servant is to be thrust outside into the darkness, out there where will be the wailing and the gnashing of teeth. This figure of the outer darkness occurs twice as a picture of punishment in the words of Jesus before this parable (Matt. 8: 12; 22: 13). It is one of the descriptions of Gehenna, like the furnace of fire (Matt. 13: 42), eternal punishment (Matt. 25: 46), the worm that dieth not (Mark 9: 48). Surely this man can represent only the nominal church member, of whom, alas, there are so many. But surely they need to be warned of the dire peril which faces a do-nothing. James calls faith like that dead (2: 26). Undoubtedly some members in our churches are dead, walking skeletons. The Parable of the Talents touches every one of us in a vital spot. By our fruits we shall be known, not by empty professions or loud claims of piety.

XII

A WALK WITH THE RISEN CHRIST

"And they said one to another, Was not our heart burning within us, while he spake to us in the way, while he opened to us the scriptures?"—LUKE 24: 32.

RENAN calls this wonderful narrative the most beautiful short story ever written. That is true, for it has one supreme advantage over all the short stories by writers like Hawthorne, Poe, Bret Harte, O. Henry, in that it is true. There is simple charm of style, but it rings true because Luke here with consummate skill pictures this walk and talk of two disciples with the Risen Christ without their knowing who their companion is till the end. Ian Maclaren, himself the author of *Beside the Bonnie Briar Bush* and other delightful Scottish stories, says that he sometimes wished that he had never read the Gospel of Luke that he might again have the joy of reading it for the first time. Certainly the proper way to enjoy this narrative is to catch the historical atmosphere of the chapter, to start with Cleopas and his fellow disciple as with sad hearts they begin the journey that Sunday afternoon to Emmaus, their home, some seven miles west of Jerusalem. Luke may have learned the story directly from Cleopas with all its picturesque detail. We need some historical imagination and to forget our later knowledge and to follow the narrative as the story unfolds itself.

1. *Two Discouraged Disciples on their Way Home on Sunday Afternoon.*

The precise identification of the town of Emmaus is not certain, whether El Kubeibeh (Plummer) or Kal-

118

oniyeh or Khamasa. We do not know the name of the
companion of Cleopas, but it is evident that they are
not apostles, though like them they disbelieved the story
of the women from the angels about the Risen Jesus.
That matters little also. " They communed with each
other of all these things which had happened." They
had heard the story of the women and the angels (verse
23) and were engaged in " lively discussion, perhaps ac-
companied with some heat. One might be sceptical, the
other more inclined to believe the story of the resurrection " (Bruce). They were conversing with one another,
a graphic picture of conversation on the greatest of
themes, the life and work of Jesus Christ, " which Cow-
per treats as a type of what true conversation should
be " (Ragg). The Greek word used here (*homileo*) is
the one from which our word " homiletics " is derived
and means to be in company with, to talk with. Originally sermons were conversational in style and so the
word was used for preaching, but not of the declam-
atory, oratorical sort.

These two disciples were opening their hearts to one
another in the midst of the gloom that had settled upon
them with the eclipse of their faith and hope when Jesus
was crucified. They felt the awe of an eclipse of the
sun. The rumours that were rife gave no solid comfort,
at least not to both of them, because they " questioned
together " about it all. They found some comfort in
going over the various incidents in the stupendous career
of Jesus. There were problems that neither could solve,
though perhaps one had some light on one phase of the
matter, the other on another. There are problems that
still baffle the best of us concerning the life and work of
Jesus of Nazareth. So we may easily sympathize with
these two puzzled disciples who were groping their way
home in the doubt of that dreadful Sunday. Neither
could explain all the difficulties and they probably disagreed on various points, but there was some relief to

their pent-up emotions in thus talking it all out with
frankness and simplicity. The mystery of Christ remained unexplained. If he was really the Messiah, as
he claimed and as they believed, why did he die? Each
had his say and each asked the other questions that he
could not answer about this tragic outcome of all their
hopes concerning a political Messiah who was to redeem
Israel and throw off the hated yoke of Rome. The
death of Jesus was the death of their hopes. Jesus remains for us the problem of the ages. The question of
Pilate is the personal problem of each of us: "What
shall I do with Jesus?" Does he square with our theological theories? Are we willing to take him as Lord,
and as Saviour from our sins?

2. A Stranger Joins Them.

"Jesus himself drew near and walked on with them,
but their eyes were restrained from recognizing him."
It is a graphic picture that Luke here draws. Why did
they not know him? Was his appearance changed? The
addition to Mark's Gospel (16: 12) says that "he was
manifested in another form unto two of them." Did he
not want to be recognized as yet? They were obsessed
with grief. Others too had difficulty at first in recognizing the glorified Christ as in the case of Mary Magdalene. We may profitably ask whether we to-day
would recognize Jesus Christ if we should suddenly see
him. John the Baptist pertinently said to the committee
sent from the Sanhedrin to investigate him: "In the
midst of you stands one whom ye know not" (John 1:
26). He was the unrecognized Christ then for men's
eyes were holden, as now, by preconceived notions of
theology, by prejudice, by self-interest, by worldly interests. If we only knew the Face of Jesus! A. J.
Gordon's *Spiritual Autobiography* tells of his dream that
he was preaching of Christ one day when he came slowly
walking down the central aisle toward the pulpit! We

have all read Tolstoy's story about Christ appearing to people in the guise of one who needed help and shelter. And thus Jesus pictured the surprise of those who at the last are commended " inasmuch as ye did it unto me," when they helped the sick and suffering.

Here the stranger overtakes the two travelers and listens to their talk as they are walking along together. Then he politely asks: " What are the words that ye are exchanging with one another as ye walk? " The word for " are exchanging " (*antiballete*) means literally to toss back and forth like a ball, a vivid picture of conversation between two. Jesus was the topic of their talk when the stranger made his appearance. Do we miss the fellowship of Christ to-day because we talk exclusively about other things? The two disciples were astonished at the stranger and " stood still looking sad " (with downcast faces). Cleopas was quick to express his surprise: " Hast thou been dwelling in Jerusalem alone and so did not come to know the things that have taken place there in these days? " In Jerusalem they knew by their own experience that there was only one topic of conversation, so that they conclude that the stranger had seen no one while in the city. But he calmly repeats his question: " What sort of things? "

3. *The Story of Jesus as Told by the Two Disciples.*

Dr. Lock thinks that the two friends were " tumbling over one another " in eagerness to tell " the things concerning Jesus the Nazarene." They give the stranger a summary of the life and work of one who " proved to be " " a prophet mighty in deed and word before God and all the people." He was commissioned by God as a prophet and accepted as such by the people. This much they still believe about him. They told also the sad outcome, his condemnation and crucifixion by the rulers of the people. The hierarchs (ecclesiastics) rejected him while the people accepted him. It was a " tragic story:

the best of men treated as the worst by the self-styled good" (Bruce). But now, alas, their dearest hopes had come to naught. They had only the Dead Sea of disappointment and despair. "But we were hoping that he was the one who was about to redeem Israel," from the yoke of Roman bondage. The Triumphal Entry seemed to be an open declaration on the part of Jesus that he was the Messiah and the crowds at the passover so understood it in glad jubilation. He was taken to be the national hope of Israel, but was betrayed by the Pharisees and Sadducees. It is now the third day (Sunday afternoon) since the death and burial of Jesus (Friday afternoon). All of us know what it is to have disappointed hopes, the accumulation of disappointments. There was one faint gleam of light to which the two disciples attach no real importance, though they mention it to the stranger. There was a flicker of excitement over the report of some women who early this very morning had found the tomb of Jesus empty and claimed that they had seen a vision of angels who said that Jesus was alive. They themselves took no stock in this rumour. It was too much a matter of women and angels for belief. They were not credulous themselves. It is true that some of the men went to the tomb and did find it empty, but they did not see Jesus or the angels. The matter was too important to decide it on the basis of the report of nervous and excitable women, one of whom, Mary Magdalene, had had seven demons cast out of her. So the two cautious and wise men, feeling superior to the women, were still in the dark and without hope as they told their story to the stranger. It was all so far only "hearsay evidence and unsatisfactory" (Plummer). When the two left Jerusalem, Mary Magdalene and the other women had not yet reported that they themselves had seen Jesus (Luke 24: 10f.), but the disciples did not believe when they did say that (John 20: 18; Mark 16: 13). The story of the resurrection still rested only on the testimony of the women about the vision of the angels.

4. The Stranger's Exposition of the Old Testament Concerning the Messiah.

"And he said unto them, O foolish men, and slow of heart to believe in all that the prophets have spoken!" There is special point in the "all" here. "Like most Jews, they remembered only the promises of the glories of the Messiah, and ignored the predictions of his suffering" (Plummer). The stranger rebuked them sadly for being stupid and dull in intellect and slow in believing. Their devotion and dismay had blinded their intellectual apprehension of the value of the testimony of the women and the angels. They were wrong in the wavering of faith and the refusal to believe the evidence. They did not understand the prophecy in the Old Testament and so disbelieved the evidence.

As a matter of fact, it was necessary for the Messiah to suffer and die and to rise again. "Behooved it not the Christ to suffer these things, and to enter into his glory?" This was strange doctrine to the two disciples who still shared the view of the Jewish leaders that the Christ, the Son of man, was to abide forever, and not be lifted up or crucified (John 12: 32–34). The suffering and death of Jesus, the chief obstacle to their faith in him as the Messiah, is here turned into proof (by his resurrection) that he is the Messiah. The stranger saw how bewildered they were at this way of looking at it. So he undertook to show that he was right in his interpretation of the Old Testament as opposed to the views of a political Messiah held by the rabbis. "And beginning from Moses and from all the prophets he interpreted to them in all the scriptures the things concerning himself!" It was marvellous exegesis, so fresh, so original, so different from the traditions of the fathers in the synagogues. The scales began to loosen from their eyes, though still clinging to them and obscuring the light. They had a strange heart-burning as they listened to this stranger prove that the prophets portrayed a suffering, dying, and glorified Messiah. Probably such prophecies as those about the seed of the woman bruising the serpent's head, types like the brazen serpent, passages like the suffering servant in Isaiah 53, were discussed. They had heretofore had only a partial view of the Messiah of their scriptures. Now they see that the Messiah is the key to the Old Testament that unlocks its mysteries, the only key that does that. But, apart from disputed passages, the stranger showed that the Old Testament predicted a Suffering Messiah such as Jesus had shown himself to be. There are those to-day who are not able to find a real Messiah in the Old Testament and deny that Jesus claimed to be the Messiah. This passage is respectfully presented to such critics who are still " foolish and slow of heart to believe." This stranger had no difficulty on that score. It was, then, still possible to believe in Jesus as the Messiah. New truth is always disturbing, but intensely stimulating. New light was dawning for the two disciples who were walking in the presence of the Light of the World without knowing it. I once had a student, a Russian Jew, who told me that, when a boy of twelve, he overheard his father saying to his mother that he, Jacob, was going to be a Christian, because (he explained) he had caught him reading the Old Testament; not the Talmud, please observe, but the Old Testament. The father was sure that the Old Testament would make Jacob a Christian, as it did. The veil was lifted from Jacob's heart when he read the New Testament after reading the Old (2 Cor. 3: 16). Jesus is the Messiah of the Old as shown in the New Covenant. The two disciples make no reply to the stranger's entrancing exposition. But it had found a place in their hearts and caused a strange burning of heart which they understood later.

5. The Stranger Makes Himself Known.

"He made as though he would go further." He was not acting a part and would certainly have gone on if he had not been invited to stay. The stranger was courteous as Jesus always is. He will not force himself upon the life of any one who is unwilling to let him come in. He may stand without and knock for entrance, but the latch-string must be pulled on the inside. Will you ask Jesus to come into your heart now? The disciples were so completely fascinated by the talk of the stranger that they were quite unwilling for him to go on. They "constrained" him by eager words of invitation: "Abide with us, for it is toward evening and the day is now far spent." It was probably the home of Cleopas or of the other. They both felt "an instinctive yearning" (Ragg), for more fellowship with this stranger. Lyte's wonderful hymn, "Abide with me, fast falls the eventide," comes from this incident. At the evening meal the stranger took the lead and presided "while they watched him, charmed and wondering." "He took the bread and blessed and breaking it he gave unto them." Instantly the scales fell from the eyes of the two disciples. "He vanished out of their sight" just as he appeared in the room in Jerusalem with closed doors (Luke 24: 36; John 20: 19, 22). It was "disappearance without physical locomotion" (Plummer). He had been with them in their walk, their talk, their meal. There is a saying ascribed to Jesus in the Logia of Jesus, "raise the stone and there thou shalt find me; cleave the wood and there am I." The two disciples looked at each other to see if the recognition was mutual, as it was. But Jesus was gone. If we only were able to recognize Christ when he is with us in our daily toil! How much sweeter and richer our tasks would be.

6. The Effect on the Two Disciples.

There was a simultaneous outburst: "Was not our

heart burning within us, while he spake to us in the way, while he opened to us the scriptures?" How slow and stupid their minds had been to lag behind their hearts! Jesus was opening the scriptures about himself and their eyes were not opening to see him. "They regard the glow in their hearts as further proof that it was indeed Jesus who was with them as they walked" (Plummer). Now they recognize him because their hearts were in tune to receive this self-revelation of Jesus. It was burning while Jesus was talking and it was burning now that he has vanished from their sight, but not from their hearts.

The women were right after all, blessings on them. There is but one thing to do. They must go back at once to Jerusalem and tell the brotherhood that they have seen the Risen Christ. The glorious fact must be told to dispel the gloom on the hearts of all. The meal can wait. No matter if night had come. At that very hour they started and found the other disciples gathered together, possibly in the home of Mary the mother of John Mark. But, before they can tell their own story to confirm the witness of the women, they are welcomed with the glad tidings: "The Lord is Risen indeed, and hath appeared to Simon." This tremendous fact has changed the whole situation. The darkness has disappeared. Joy has taken the place of gloom. All that they can do now is to fill the cup of joy full to overflowing by telling their own thrilling experience, for they had a story to tell. So have we if we let Jesus come into our hearts and go with us the whole way. This is the message that the world is hungry for, the experience of grace in our own lives. Let Christ reveal himself to you and then tell it to others.

XIII

PAUL'S FIVE EPISTLES IN ONE

"Ye are our epistle, written in our hearts, known and read of all men."—2 CORINTHIANS 3: 2.

PAUL is the greatest letter writer of all time, because of the subject matter, the directness of style, and the wisdom of his words. They have permanent value for us because they met the actual needs of men who were trying to live for and like Jesus Christ, their Lord and Saviour. Paul was not a professional letter writer nor a *littérateur* in any sense. He followed no rules of rhetoric, but the law of love. He used the vernacular Greek of the first century, but the language of an educated man all ablaze with passion for Christ. Some of the noblest passages in all literature occur in these letters as they flash forth from Paul's mind and heart. Dr. James Stalker has a volume entitled *The Four Men* (the man as people in general see him, his reputation; the man that his intimate friends think he is; the man that he thinks himself to be; the man that God knows him to be). One might also add a fifth, the man that his wife and children take him to be. So here we may take the word epistle in five senses. Paul plays with the word epistle or letter and turns it round like the facets of a diamond that we may see it from every angle.

1. *The Epistle on Paper.*

We need not press the distinction drawn by Deissmann between letter and epistle as that between a familiar and a more formal writing. The Greek word *epistolē* can mean either. The word comes from the verb meaning to send to one. Paul's letters are either personal, public or both. They met immediate needs, but often were to be read in the meetings of the church (Col. 4: 16), and were meant for instruction and guidance (2 Thess. 2: 15; 3: 12). Paul probably wrote on papyrus as was the custom at that time save for larger documents which were written on parchment (2 Tim. 4: 13). Clay tablets were once the common form of letters and thousands have been preserved at Tel El Amarna and in Babylonia. Pieces of pottery were used by the poor or even bark or wood. Stone has always been common for inscriptions. So Paul alludes to " tables of stone " and to " ink."

Paul feels sure that the Corinthians can read what he has written to them. " For we write no other things unto you, than what ye read or even acknowledge, and I hope ye will acknowledge unto the end." Paul's language was simple and clear and even those unable to read could understand it when read aloud. There was a higher ratio of literacy in the Græco-Roman world at this time than ever before and for many centuries afterwards (as J. P. Mahaffy shows in his books). Even Paul's enemies in Corinth admitted that his " letters are weighty and strong, but his bodily presence is weak and his speech of no account " (2 Cor. 10: 10). They made this charge, Paul says, to discount the power of his letters to the church. But " I shall not be put to shame, that I may not seem as if I would terrify you by my letters " (verse 9). He will do as he has written, they will find out. The charge was also made that Paul wrote " shuffling letters, in which one has to read between the lines in order to see that what he seems to say is not what he really means " (Plummer). His epistles and his motives were misunderstood. There is no hidden meaning in my letters, Paul means to say. He means precisely what his words affirm. Denney laments this " disgrace to human nature that a man so open, so truthful, so brave,

should be put to his defence on a charge of underhand
dealing " in his letters. It is amazing how ready some
people are to misunderstand what one says in print or
in speech. They misunderstood Paul in Thessalonica
and misrepresented him in Corinth. False charges were
made against Jesus and against Stephen before the Sanhedrin. What people see in a letter or book or hear in a
sermon or address depends partly on the prejudices
behind the eyes and ears. It is easy to see what is not
there as any proof-reader can testify to his sorrow. When
the book is printed the errors glare at you. They were
there all the while, but were not seen. There is such a
thing as a *lapsus pennæ, linguæ, oculi, mentis*. It is so
often that we do not catch clearly what we read. Sir W.
Robertson Nicoll once had a fine editorial in *The British
Weekly* on " Books that We Think We have Read." The
Bible was the first one in his list. My experience as a
teacher of the New Testament confirms this position.
The obvious things slip through the memory like water
through our fingers. And yet reading is one of the
noblest joys and blessings of life. What will or can take
the place of good books? Not the daily paper, not the
radio, not the movie. It is good to be able to read.

Paul in his old age in prison will long for his books,
especially the parchments, books that he knew almost
by heart. The Bible in one sense is God's love letter to
the world. When we get letters from our loved ones,
we often read them many times to be sure that we get
all the meaning that is in them, sometimes love delicately
put like the aroma of a rose. There is always danger
that cold print will not properly represent what we
meant to say. That is why new translations of the Bible
are continually coming out. Words fade and lose their
original meaning. So a constant struggle goes on between the new and the old. The vernacular is better
understood, but it must not be vulgar. It is sometimes
hard to express what one feels in mere words even when

there is the gift of expression, of style, of power with
the pen. Paul longed to be with the Galatians again
that he might change his tone of voice (Gal. 4: 20),
that they might see and hear him again. That is the
power of preaching and nothing will ever take the place
of the living voice of the real preacher of Christ as he
opens his heart to men.

2. The Epistle in Paul's Heart.

"Ye are our epistle, written in our hearts." This
epistle lies behind the one written in ink on papyrus or
parchment and despatched to the Corinthians. Paul
loved the Corinthians and his love prompted him to
write his love letters to them. He did love them even
when he wrote sharp things to them. " For out of much
affliction and anguish of heart I wrote unto you with
many tears; not that ye might be made sorry, but that
ye might know the love which I have more abundantly
unto you " (2 Cor. 2: 4). The more he loved them, the
more tears he shed because he had to write so sternly
to them. The divisions in Corinth gave Paul heartaches
and he was even sorry " that that epistle made you
sorry, though for a season " (7: 8), " for ye were made
sorry after a godly sort, that ye might suffer loss by
us in nothing " (verse 9). Chrysostom says that Paul's
love for the Corinthians made him sing their praises in
spite of their shortcomings. Paul is moved " by the
memory of his labours among them which had left an
indelible impression upon his heart " (Bernard). This
" letter written on Paul's heart was not open to the
world " (ibid.), but it was there to stay, come what
might. " I say it not to condemn you; for I have said
before, that ye are in our hearts to die together, and
live together " (7: 3). Nothing can stop Paul's love for
them as nothing can make Christ cease loving us (Rom.
8: 38f.). " Ye are our glorying " (2 Cor. 1: 14). Ye
are my epistle of commendation, Paul means. " You

are the commendatory letter which I show, when I am asked for my credentials " (Denney). You acknowledged me before, you acknowledge me now, you will acknowledge me (1: 13f.).

Each of us has " heart epistles," names of loved ones engraved there forever, cherished memories of childhood and of old age. There are holy places in every heart, secret recesses of the soul. This tablet of the heart is imperishable. Paul probably was not thinking of the plate of pure gold that Aaron wore as he went into the holy place with the words " Holy to Jehovah " (Exodus 28: 36f.). It is not the idea of intercession here, but of pure affection. Love begets love. The pastor who loves his people will be loved by them.

There are epistles in our hearts that we never wrote, letters that we meant to write to mother or friend and never did. Now it is too late. There are words of love and appreciation that we meant to speak and did not utter. Perhaps we started to say them and faltered at some interruption or flutter of the heart and now it is too late to say them. So also there are words that we did speak in a moment of rashness or of petulance that we would give a kingdom to recall, but they were spoken and they were heard and cut to the heart one that we loved and love still. Even our best loved ones do not always rightly read the epistle in the heart. There are things written in the heart that only God reads and fully knows. Jesus does understand us and bids us to come to him with all our heart troubles. Paul pleads with the Corinthians to open their hearts to him (7: 2) for his heart was enlarged toward them and his mouth was open unto them (6: 11). He asked for perfect sympathy and understanding of his deep and abiding love.

3. The Epistle in Paul's Life.

" For our glorying is this, the testimony of our con-

science, that in holiness and sincerity of God, not in
fleshly wisdom, but in the grace of God, we behaved
ourselves in the world, and more abundantly to you-
ward " (1: 12). Paul's life in Corinth for two years was
an open book. In a city so wicked as Corinth there was
ample opportunity for Paul " to use the world's underhand and slippery methods " (Plummer), but he had
not done so, as the brethren in Corinth knew full well.
The Corinthians in part at least recognized Paul as
their " ground of glorying " (2 Cor. 1: 14). Paul's life
in Corinth was the epistle that all read and noted carefully. That is true of the preacher to-day. People will
read and watch his life who will not listen to his sermons.
They watch his steps as their Bible and accept or reject
Christ accordingly. Paul needed no letter or recommendation to the Corinthians (2 Cor. 3: 1). Apollos
brought one from Priscilla and Aquila in Ephesus when
he went to Corinth (Acts 18: 17) and he deserved it.
People are sometimes tempted to be polite enough to
give letters of recommendation to one unfit or even
unworthy. It is a sad blunder. We wish to be generous,
but we must also be honest. Mere flattery at such a
time is a wrong to all concerned. Wherever Paul might
need recommendation, it was certainly not at Corinth.
" If to others I am not an apostle, yet at least I am
to you; for the seal of mine apostleship are ye in the
Lord " (1 Cor. 9: 2). Most of the believers in Corinth
still say of Paul that " we are your glorying " (2 Cor.
1: 14). Some at Corinth misread the epistle of Paul's
life, misconstrued his motives, slandered him shamefully.
They accused him of living according to the flesh, of
being a coward when in Corinth and only brave in his
letters, of going beyond his province in trying to regulate
their affairs anyhow, of not being a genuine apostle
because he was not one of the Twelve, of declining to
take pay for his preaching because he knew he was an
impostor, of being after their money indirectly through

Titus in the collection for the poor saints in Jerusalem (10: 1–15; 12: 14–18). And yet Paul went on loving these people and won the church back to love and loyalty.

4. The Epistle in the Hearts of the Readers.

"Ye are our epistle, ministered by us, written not with ink, but with the Spirit of the living God; not in tables of stone, but in tables that are hearts of flesh" (3: 3). The Spirit of God wrote this epistle in each of their hearts. Paul was the preacher and the writer of letters to them. But the Spirit of God writes the burning message in their hearts. This is the work of grace on tables of the heart. Some letters are marked "personal," not meant for other eyes. There are men who have emotional power of a high order, who touch our hearts. There is a wondrous mystery in human speech that touches the springs of action in the heart. And now the radio adds to the mystery still more when without wire or any contact but the air or ether we can with proper transmitter and receiver, tune in and hear voices from all over the world, human voices with messages light and grave as the case may be. There is no longer cause for wonder, if there was any, that the Spirit of the living God can and does touch our hearts when we are in tune with the Infinite. Here it "is the mystical imprint of the Divine Spirit in their hearts, conveyed through Paul's ministrations" (Bernard). This is the wonder and the glory of preaching whether by voice or by letter. Jesus wrote no letters or books, but his words live and burn in millions of hearts to-day. Plato in *Phædrus* tells of the teacher who does not write his words in perishable ink, but stamps them on a congenial soul that will pass them on to others. The joy of the preacher of Christ is to see hearts born again under the power of the gospel, to see Christ formed in the soul (Gal. 4: 19). For this joy the greatest spirits

of earth have turned away from the appeal of money,
or earthly power. Paul rejoiced in the picture of Christ,
the Image of God who shined in their hearts for the
illumination of the knowledge of God in the face of
Jesus Christ (2 Cor. 4: 6). It made his heart sing for
joy to call up the vision of the faces in Corinth that
shone with the light of heaven in the darkness around
them.

5. *The Epistle in the Lives of the Readers.*

"Known and read of all men, being made manifest
that ye are an epistle of Christ" (3: 2f.). This is the
epistle that the world read in Corinth. So it is to-day.
The Bible that the world reads is the lives of the Christians. These pages are scanned daily. "The letter
written on the heart of the Corinthians by Christ
through Paul's ministry was patent to the world's observation, as it was reflected in their Christian mode of
life. Facts speak louder than words" (Bernard).
They are the living epistles of the living God. Men
judged whether the epistle of Christ was written in their
hearts by seeing whether they could read it in their lives.
It is not certain whether Paul means that they are the
epistle of Christ in the sense that they belong to Christ,
were Christ's message to men, or a letter that tells about
Christ. As a matter of fact, each view is true. The
new heart was the work of the Spirit of Christ as the
new life is only possible in Christ. Certainly we belong
to Christ. Surely men will judge of Christ by what
they see in us in contrast with the world in which we
live. Emerson long ago put this truth crisply when he
said that what one is thunders so loud that we do not
hear what he says. In a real sense we are all "miniature
Christs," very dim and small and imperfect, to be sure.
And yet it is forever true that men eye us and see if
we have been with Jesus and bear the marks of his
ownership and likeness. There is no escaping this

responsibility. It is our chief opportunity of service for Christ. The Spirit of the living God does find access to the secret places of one's soul. Touched by that Spirit, we should lead new lives because we have new hearts. " The true epistles of Christ to the world are not those which are expounded in pulpits; they are not even the gospel in which Christ himself lives and moves before us; they are living men and women, on the tables of whose hearts the Spirit of the living God, ministered by a true evangelist, has engraved the likeness of Christ Himself " (Denney). That is " the Divine writing which is the guarantee of all else." When men turn in eager longing to read the epistle of Christ in your life and mine what do they read?

XIV

ON PAROLE ONE YEAR MORE

"Lord, let it alone this year also."—LUKE 13: 8.

INTERPRETATION of Providence is one of the common habits of men. The constant reminders in the daily papers of crime and accident, of sickness and death, force upon us the manifold problems of our complex life. The radio has intensified this age-old mystery. Luke has here brought together an Outrage, an Accident, and a Parable that illustrate in a vivid way modern living conditions. They are given only by this Gospel and he connects them directly with the preceding events in chapter 12 " at that very season." The discussion in chapter 12 was on the subject of judgment with the eager language of Christ for the kindling of the fire and the baptism of blood (12: 49f.).

1. *The Outrage of Pilate.*

Apparently some people, who were not in the crowds addressed by Jesus in chapter 12, came up of a sudden with a piece of news which they eagerly told Jesus. They stepped up to his side to be the first to proclaim to Jesus this latest horror that Pontius Pilate had wrought. The incident is not told by Josephus or any other historian save Luke, but it is wholly of a piece with the picture of Pilate in Josephus. Pilate had ruthlessly slain some Galilean pilgrims as they were approaching the temple with their sacrifices at one of the feasts. There may have been some fanatical act of rebellion that gave Pilate, who was present at the feast with his Roman soldiers to preserve order, an excuse for ordering the execution of some of the offenders. It was a horrible thing, for the blood of the victims was literally mingled with that of the slaughtered beasts in the sacrifices. This conduct of Pilate toward Galileans may be one of the causes of the enmity between Herod Antipas (Tetrarch of Galilee) and Pilate which Luke also mentions (23: 12). Keim suggests that the arrest of Barabbas took place at this time. The informants may have had no motive other than to tell Jesus the news of this latest horror and to get his reaction toward the tyranny of the Roman government as illustrated by Pilate. The Galileans, in particular, were restive under the yoke of Rome and the war with Rome will break out there first of all. Long before this near Bethsaida Julias Jesus had to send away the excited Galilæan multitudes who wanted to take him by force to Jerusalem and make him king instead of Cæsar (John 6: 14f.).

This Galilean tragedy gives an occasion for Jesus to make some pertinent comments on current events. There are two extremes about the use of current topics in preaching. Some preachers make their sermons almost wholly on the latest newspaper sensation. They get their texts still from the Bible, but their sermons from the newspaper or the radio. They give people on Sunday, who are hungry for the gospel of eternal life, a rehash of scandal, crime, politics, or business, subjects with which the people are already surfeited. Broadus used to say that in such cases, if the text had the smallpox, the sermon would not catch it. They are so far apart and disconnected. Jesus did find fault with the Pharisees for not being able to read the signs of the times though they claimed to be experts on signs about the weather (Matt. 16: 3). It is all right to be interested in news, but the best and freshest news in the world is the gospel of Christ properly understood and rightly told. The very word " gospel " means good news.

Too many are like the Athenians who had no time for
anything but something newer than the last scrap of
sensation (Acts 17: 21). These transmitters of the latest
item in the long list of Pilate's atrocities were all agog
with excitement just like newsboys in our cities crying
" extra." What did Jesus think of such conduct by the
Governor?

Jesus could have passed by such a dangerous topic,
but for once he had something to say about it.   The
sermon topics in the metropolitan pulpits as announced
on Saturday in Chicago and New York are often
evanescent and unimportant with no appeal to the soul
of man.   There was an old preacher who once apologized
for his choice of spiritual themes on the ground that,
while so many were preaching for the times, he might
be excused for preaching for eternity.   Jesus at once
turns the popular interest about the incident to good
account for the benefit of the informers and all the
hearers whether their sympathies were with the Galileans or with Pilate.   These Galileans were not " sinners
above all the Galileans " as many supposed, according
to a common doctrine of the Jews that all calamity was
the result of one's own sin.   Job's miserable comforters
gave him the full benefit of this type of theology.   Even
the disciples asked Jesus in the case of the man born
blind whether he or his parents had sinned as the cause
of his blindness (John 9: 2).   Disease is sometimes the
result of one's own sin, but by no means always, as the
Master showed.   We need not argue whether these informers desired Christ to make a protest against the
conduct of Pilate or to endorse their theology that these
particular Galileans were dreadful culprits and deserved
their fate.   He makes no comment about Pilate's conduct, but does brush aside the inference of the great guilt
of the victims of Pilate's cruelty.   He applies the result
of the outrage to the audience before him as proof of the
uncertainty of life and the need of immediate change

to be ready for death. " I tell you, Nay; but, except ye repent, ye shall all likewise perish." This is what matters for us all, to be ready for death in whatever form and at whatever time it comes. The thing for us to do is to be ready now before it is too late. Jesus draws a lesson for the living from the fate of the dead. This is the chief value of funeral sermons, not merely the comfort of the sorrowing ones, important as that is. Whatever the guilt of the Galileans may be, our guilt will bring condemnation on us unless we repent before it is too late. And the hour of death is too late, Jesus plainly means. In the destruction of Jerusalem, forty years after this Josephus tells us, Titus " sprinkled the holy altar with their blood." That will be terrible, but meanwhile death in some form confronted all who heard Jesus then. That is the lesson of Pilate's outrage for them and for us. Jesus is our only hope in life and death.

2. The Accident at Siloam.

To illustrate the application of the lesson from the outrage of Pilate, Jesus turns to the example of the recent accident at Siloam with which they were all familiar. He thus makes plain his previous lesson. He knew how to use current events to point a lesson. The Pool of Siloam has been clearly located in Jerusalem (John 9: 7). Ewald thinks that this accident happened to eighteen of the workmen that Pilate employed in building the aqueducts in Jerusalem. He met the expense of this by using " the sacred treasure " or " Corban " (Josephus, *Wars*, ii. 9.4) to the disgust and indignation of the people of Jerusalem. Josephus says that these " offenders," literally " debtors," the workmen paid with the sacred funds, were under obligation to pay back to the temple what they had received from Pilate. But at any rate these Judean workmen were moral debtors to God like the sinners from Galilee slain by

Pilate, but not more so than the other dwellers in Jerusalem. The fact that the tower fell on them does not prove that they were worse sinners or greater debtors than others. It was a catastrophe at Siloam, but one that is likely to happen to all men. Surely the railroad, the automobile, the airplane, the steamship, the coal mines of modern life, all emphasize this fact, quite apart from such convulsions of nature as earthquakes, tornadoes, volcanoes, fires.

The interpretation of calamity is a knotty subject. It is easy enough to say, when only others are involved, that it is a righteous judgment of God for their sins or mistakes. But when the blow falls upon us, as in a financial crash, we demur, and regard it all as a misfortune, not a condemnation. We forget that God according to Jesus sends rain upon the just and the unjust alike. In the Parable of the Rich Man and Lazarus, riches in this life fell to the wicked man and poverty to the good man. In the other world these conditions are precisely reversed. In the two current incidents touched upon by the Master here, he does not say that their lot or fate was an index to their real character. They were all sinners beyond a doubt, but their misfortunes did not come upon them because of this fact. According to this saying of Christ some good men might be involved in the two calamities here mentioned. Accidents to-day in travel and industrial life are far ahead of the loss of life in war. Good men and women suffer in such accidents often because of the acts of wicked men. Drinking drivers of automobiles take many lives and go practically unpunished. It is idle to blame God for the carelessness and reckless criminal acts of men. The good along with the bad are victims in accidents.

Christ draws the same lesson from this accident that he did from Pilate's outrage. It is the lesson of readiness for death. "Except ye repent, ye shall all likewise perish." There is a difference in tense here in the verb for " repent," the aorist for immediate action rather than the present for continued attitude in verse 3. The point is one needed everywhere to-day, repentance while there is opportunity. Accident and life insurance agencies are urgent with their statistics about life and death. They have incontestable data to clinch their arguments for instant action. And they are right. But men grow callous and hard-hearted before the pleas for instant action in the case of repentance toward God. *Mañana* (to-morrow) will do. There is plenty of time. We will risk another day, another month, another year before we settle this greatest of all problems, our relation with Almighty God. " Under the ruins of your fortress " (Holtzmann) Jesus pleads for immediate repentance before it is too late. Christ is the expert on the knowledge of God and man's relation to him. He is the Son of God who has come to reveal God's love to men. No evangelist in a revival ever made a more pointed and fervent plea than the Master does here for instant action. What is your answer to the warning of the Son of God?

3. *A Parable of Life from the Fig Tree.*

Christ here takes a familiar object to illustrate the same lesson. Mark (11: 22–25) and Matthew (21: 18–22) give the account of the barren fig tree that was cursed and withered because of its barrenness, a powerful object lesson at the close of the Master's work in Jerusalem. Luke does not give that incident, but does tell this parable with the same point. The two accounts in no way contradict one another. Only the parable comes first in the history and sets forth " the long-suffering and the severity of God " (Plummer) with the Jewish nation and with individuals also. It was common to have a fig tree in the corner of a vineyard, as in Tuscan vineyards olive trees grow. " The fig tree ripeneth her green figs, and the vines are in blossom "

(Song of Sol. 2: 13). Perhaps Jesus means that the
Jews should understand that God is not solely concerned
with them, as they were so apt to think. The parable
continues the previous warnings. A fig tree year after
year continues barren. The three years are to be counted
from the time the fig tree would normally be expected
to bear. There is, of course, no allusion to the length
of Christ's ministry. That is merely accidental coin-
cidence. No mystic meaning may be given to the number " three years." A long time God had been looking
for fruit from the Jewish nation. " The tree had been
fruitless long before he began to preach, and it was not
cut down until forty years after He ceased to do so "
(Plummer). But it was a time of crisis for Israel as
it is for each of us to-day. Every nation, every city,
every person has to meet the test of fruit bearing.
" By their fruits ye shall know them," says Jesus.

In disgust the owner ordered the barren fig tree cut
down. " Cut it out root and branch. Why does it make
the ground idle? " The vinedresser shows keen interest
in sparing the fig tree. He pleads for one year more.
We need not worry whether Jesus is the vinedresser or
not. " Lord, let it alone this year also, till I dig about
it, and dung it." Let me try one more year to make
the fig tree count. Then, if it bears no fruit, cut it out.
So one more year is granted the fig tree.

This is a solemn lesson for us all, for nations, for
cities. What is the use of a big city if it merely fills
up space and is a cesspool of iniquity? Judgment came
to Sodom and Gomorrah, to Nineveh and Babylon.
There is no value in a long life that is barren and fruitless. Robertson Nicoll wrote a stirring book called
The Round of the Clock in which many striking achieve-
ments are shown to be the work of young men. The
Master himself was less than thirty-five when crucified on Calvary. New Year resolutions are all right,
but there should be some performance and not mere

promise. In the end of the day it is fruit that counts and that abides. Alas, if the harvest is past, the summer is ended, and we are not saved. The withered fig tree, like this one in the parable, had leaves, but nothing else. The lesson that Jesus drew for the disciples was to have faith in God, faith that will remove mountains of difficulty from across our path.

Life is God's gift to us, a mystery and a wonder. Let us use it for his glory. There is joy in life, but the chief joy in it is in making others happy. Life brings opportunities to do good for God and men. To waste life is sin. Selfishness is squandering life's health and wealth. Repentance is to change one's life before it is too late. Time is God's gift for this very purpose. The present is the only time that we actually possess. It brings privilege and peril. There is no escaping the penalty of a wasted life. That debt God and nature require that we pay. Finally the fruitless tree is cut out of the way and another is planted in its place. The reward of eternal life means more life, abundant life here and hereafter, rich beyond measure, unending life with Christ and those that love him. If we fail to bear fruit after one more chance, the parole is over and the doom of the useless fig tree is sealed. You know Browning's story of Pippa, the little mill girl who sings through the streets of Asolo as she wanders hither and thither on her one day's holiday. She says, " O day, if I squander a wavelet of thee, a mite of my twelve hours treasure! " Yet little knows she when the day is past that she has touched half a dozen lives and blessed them. Now is the day of salvation for each of us and the hour for blessing some life as we pass on.

XV

JONAH THE UNWILLING MISSIONARY

"Arise, go to Nineveh, that great city, and cry against it; for their wickedness is come up before me."—JONAH 1: 2.

IT was in the eighth century B. C. during the reign of Jeroboam II that Jonah lived and prophesied (2 Kings 14: 25). Little is told about his life apart from the book that bears his name. No specific claim is made in the story that Jonah himself wrote it. The prayer in chapter 2 is in the first person. We are not concerned with that point, but only with the life of Jonah as there portrayed. The prophets were used of God to stir the people and to warn them of the impending punishment for their sins. Jonah was one of these messengers of God and a very human one at that.

1. Jonah's Great Mission.

" The word of the Lord came unto Jonah the son of Amittai." That is an event in the life of any man, even though a prophet of God. It was an event when " the word of God came unto John the son of Zacharias in the wilderness " (Luke 3: 2). It demands attention whenever God puts a task upon one's shoulders. The call to you and me may not come by direct inspiration as it did to Jonah and to John, but the path of duty may lie plainly before us, whether the call comes by ordinary or extraordinary means.

In Jonah's case the demand was that he go to Nineveh, that great city, and cry against it. The wickedness of Nineveh, the greatest city on earth at that time, was rising before the Lord like the smoke belching forth from our modern cities to-day. There is not a city now that escapes the notice of God, nor a single community, for that matter. It is not a pleasant task to cry against a great city to its face. It is much easier to stand off and rail against the vices of the modern Babylons and Ninevehs. Jonah knew that it was a dangerous and an unpopular thing to do that in Nineveh. Nathan did have courage to stand before David and say: "Thou art the man." Elijah was bold before Ahab on Mount Carmel, but he ran like a deer from Jezebel and sat under the juniper tree in despair. There were false prophets in plenty with soft voices and smooth sayings to please princes. Jonah did not relish the call that came to him.

2. *Jonah Shirking His Duty.*

His heart sank within him at the prospect of facing the great city and exposing its sins. Many a preacher since Jonah's day has had a like experience. It is naïvely said that Jonah got into a ship at Joppa to go with the sailors "unto Tarshish from the presence of Jehovah." It was as if God did not dwell in Spain. Many a man has gone to the west from his crimes and his loved ones and friends as if God and duty were not to be found out west. But they found out their mistake sooner or later. The eye of God is always upon us even in the dark and in the haunts of sins. Hugh Redwood has found God in the underworld of London, as his wonderful book, *God in the Slums*, shows.

Jonah paid his fare like a man, because he was doing what he wanted to do. People, even in emergencies and in time of depression, have money for what they want to do, for chewing-gum, for cosmetics, for tobacco, for drink, when they have none for God and his kingdom of grace. Besides, it was a long, expensive and terrible trip to Nineveh along the edge of the desert with many perils. But it was a lovely sea voyage to Tarshish.

But God saw Jonah all the same and all the time and knew of his wilful disobedience. God sent a great wind that raised a tempest and soon the boat was tossed like a ball and the mariners were afraid. That is always a bad sign when the sailors become frightened. They cast overboard many things. Each sailor called upon his god for help. Plenty of people have no use for God till serious trouble comes and then they cry to him in terror, a poor sort of praying certainly. But Jonah lay fast asleep down in the depths of the ship. He had gone down there trying to smother his conscience for what he was doing. The shipmaster roused him roughly: " What meanest thou, O sleeper? Arise, call upon thy God, if so be that he will think upon us that we perish not." Perhaps they had heard of Jehovah as God of the Jews. The other gods had all failed them. Jonah had not gotten away from the presence of God. They cast lots to see who was the cause of the peril in which they were. The lot fell on Jonah and finally he confessed that he was guilty of trying to flee from God and his command to go to Nineveh. They did not know what to do till Jonah himself proposed that they throw him overboard lest they all perish. The men did it with much pleading that Jehovah would not punish them for Jonah's death if he were really innocent.

But God had prepared a great fish, not here called a whale (the word in Matt. 12: 40 means sea-monster), that swallowed Jonah. This miracle has created a deal of speculation through the ages. Fish have been found with the bodies of men in them, but the men were dead. Jonah could only survive in such a place by the power of God. We have precisely the same problem in the case of Daniel in the lions' den and the men in the fiery furnace. God can do what he wishes to do. Some take it as pure legend. Others regard it as a parable and not meant to be taken as literal history. Jesus spoke of the sign of Jonah as illustrating his own resurrection from the dead (Matt. 12: 40f.). Jonah now found out to his sorrow what it meant to disobey God's command.

3. Jonah Brought Back to God.

He was down in the deep waters in the belly of the fish three days and then Jonah prayed to God, a thing he refused to do in the ship. "Out of the belly of Sheol cried I." He seemed to be in hell itself down "in the heart of the seas." "All thy waves and thy billows passed over me." "The waters compassed me about, even to the soul; the deep was round about me; the weeds were wrapped about my head. I went down to the bottoms of the mountains." It took all this to bring Jonah to a realization of his sins. It takes more than this to bring some men and women back to God. They go so far and sink so low that they defy God. They feel at home in the dens and sinks of shame and have renounced home with all its hallowed ties and defame the very name of God. But Jonah now had enough of his wilful rebellion. "When my soul fainted within me, I remembered Jehovah; and my prayer came in unto thee into thy holy temple." At last Jonah is ready to say, "I will pay that which I have vowed." He is willing to go to Nineveh now. He is humbled at last and he had plenty of time to meditate. What did it take to bring you back to God when you wandered away? Many a soul has tried to flee from God. Preachers have sometimes fought a call to preach till middle life. God saw that Jonah's heart was now changed and made the fish give up Jonah on dry land.

4. Jonah Responding to the Call of God.

"And the word of Jehovah came unto Jonah a second time." That does not always happen. It would not have happened now but for the change in Jonah's attitude toward God. "Arise, go unto Nineveh, that great city, and preach unto it the preaching that I bid thee."

The slight change in the language is a direct reference
to the first command that Jonah had disregarded and a
sharp reminder that he must obey this time. Jonah is
willing now and goes " according to the word of Jehovah." He went a day's journey into Nineveh. This
street preacher had a short and strange message that
must have jarred upon the ears of the people coming
from this man of another race: " Yet forty days, and
Nineveh shall be overturned." He kept repeating his
weird words till " the people of Nineveh believed God;
and they proclaimed a fast, and put on sackcloth, from
the greatest of them even to the least of them." This
was a new experience for Jonah. Many of the prophets
proclaimed God's will to Israel and the people neglected
all of them. Jeremiah, for instance, delivered his long
messages through the years to the same people who
turned deaf ears to it all. But here the people of a
whole city, a heathen city at that, believed the terrible
words of judgment and were prostrate before God. The
message of Jonah even reached the king who was likewise deeply moved by it. He proclaimed a fast for man
and beast in view of the impending calamity: " And
let them cry mightily unto God: yea, let them turn every
one from his evil way, and from the violence that is in
his hands. Who knoweth whether God will not turn
and repent, and turn away from his fierce anger, that
we perish not? " The conduct of this king is remarkable from every point of view. He knows better than
any one the violence and evil in his own city, but he
refuses to cover it up. Here is a case where the ruler
of the city refuses to condone evil-doers and calls upon
all to turn away from their evil ways. The curse of
American cities has been precisely this, that the officers
of the law are so often in league with the law-breakers
and for bribes refuse to punish them. The helpless
people find themselves preyed upon by the very men
whom they have chosen to protect them from the under-

world. Surely no missionary in all the ages was ever
so successful in bringing a wicked city to its knees before
God. And this missionary had been unwilling to go to
Nineveh! And now his message of doom was believed
by all including the king! And yet some men wonder
if it pays to send missionaries to the heathen. Does it
pay to have preachers at home? " God saw their works,
that they turned from their evil way." Here was
" reform " with a vengeance. There was never such a
cleaning of Augean stables as this. " God repented of
the evil that he said he would do unto them; and he
did it not." And no wonder. Did ever a city before
or since turn round like this? Surely Jonah would feel
repaid for coming now when he had saved a whole city.

5. Jonah's Disappointment at God's Mercy.

" But it displeased Jonah exceedingly, and he was
angry." Instead of rejoicing at this glorious result, he
got angry and flew into a rage with God himself. He
dared even to justify his former disobedience: " I pray
thee, O Jehovah, was not this my saying when I was
yet in my country? Therefore I hasted to flee unto
Tarshish! " So quickly in his anger has he forgotten
the experience in the big fish. " For I knew that thou
art a gracious God, and merciful, slow to anger, and
abundant in loving-kindness, and repentest thee of the
evil." That was the language of impertinence and rebellion against the very character of God. " Therefore
now, O Jehovah, take I beseech thee, my life from me;
for it is better for me to die than to live." That is the
climax of bitter resentment against the love and mercy
of God who had sent him to Nineveh. God patiently
said to Jonah: " Doest thou well to be angry? " Jonah
refused to answer. What was the matter with him? He
cared more for the vindication of his own proclamation
of the ruin of the city than for the lives of the people.
He sensitively and foolishly imagined that these very

people, whose lives had been spared, would call him a false prophet. He had said that yet forty days and Nineveh would be destroyed and now that was not going to happen. Jonah felt himself put in a bad light with the people. He had rather have his way than save souls. He had rather have his way than God's way. He actually felt himself superior to God. If he could not have his own way, he preferred death to life. He thought he knew better how to run the kingdom of God than God himself. So soon has Jonah forgotten the storm and the fish.

So in a huff he " went out of the city and sat on the east side of the city, and there made him a booth, and sat under it in the shade, till he might see what would become of the city." What a picture for us all! There was still a chance that God might destroy the city and vindicate Jonah's preaching. At any rate he would give God a chance before he finally condemned him! God was kind to Jonah as he is to us all. He treated Jonah as a spoilt child as many a preacher has been. He gave him an object lesson. He caused a gourd to grow quickly over the booth to be a shade over his head against the hot rays of the sun. Jonah was exceedingly glad of the gourd vine over his head. Then a worm in the morning cut the gourd and it withered and " the sun beat upon the head of Jonah, that he fainted, and requested for himself that he might die, and said, It is better for me to die than to live." Here he is again upset, this time over a mere trifle and ready to fling his life away for a whim. Then God speaks to Jonah: " Doest thou well to be angry for the gourd? " Imagine the reply of Jonah to the Lord: " I do well to be angry, even unto death." Some people, like Jonah, become sulky when they cannot have their way in every detail of life. Jonah now, for this second offense, deserved to die, but God was merciful to him as he was to the people of Nineveh. God plainly applies the kindergarten lesson from the gourd to Jonah who grieved over the loss of the gourd vine. " Should I not have regard for Nineveh, that great city, wherein are more than sixscore thousand persons that cannot discern between their right hand and their left hand; and also much cattle? " There was no answer from Jonah to this telling and overwhelming question. He was silenced, if not convinced. Please note God's pity for the cattle also as well as for the ignorant people of Nineveh and for the stubborn and wilful prophet. Surely we are all wandering sheep, preachers and all. What a call is the story of Jonah and Nineveh to sinners to-day to turn to God while his mercy still holds out toward us all.

XVI

SAMSON: PLAYING WITH TEMPTATION

"But he knew not that the Lord was departed from him."
—JUDGES 16: 20.

SAMSON is a character full of strange contradictions. He was the strongest man in physical exploits, a regular Hercules in muscular energy, and weak as water in morality. He became a weak strong man like many a modern pugilist. He became grossly sensual and yet in that rude time, when the Philistines dominated the land, he ruled Israel sporadically for twenty years. His career will repay study in these days of Freudian obsession and rejection of moral control.

1. *He Was a Child of Promise and of Consecration.*

The story of Samson, given at considerable length in Judges (13–16), relates that an angel of the Lord revealed to the wife of Manoah of the tribe of Dan, that she was to have a son who was to be " a Nazirite unto God " from his birth. Meanwhile the mother was to drink no wine or strong drink and to eat no unclean food. All proper prenatal precautions were to be taken to give this child of promise a fair and a fine chance of service to the Lord. Manoah and his wife were deeply impressed by this manifestation of God's favour and presence. The child was named Samson. He " grew and the Lord blessed him. And the Spirit of the Lord began to move him in Mahaneh-dan, between Zorah and Eshtaol." Beyond a doubt we are to understand that this young man was a chosen vessel of the Lord " to save Israel out of the hands of the Philistines." " No razor shall come upon his head." He was a Nazirite and was not to take strong drink of any kind. The law of the Nazirite is given in Numbers 6: 1–21 and included total abstinence from strong drink and avoidance of dead bodies and " he shall be holy; he shall let the locks of his hair grow long " (Num. 6: 5). The long hair was the outward sign and symbol of his consecration to the Lord. Some hold that Samuel was also a Nazirite, though it is not so stated. Amos (2: 11f.) refers to Nazirites in his day. They were not necessarily saintly men, as we understand the term to-day. Samson's vow of consecration to the Lord did not include purity of sex relations in his case. It sometimes happens that rigid restrictions in one line induce license in other ways. A man may wholly abstain from strong drink, as he should, and yet be unscrupulous in his use of money and unreliable in his relations with women. It is to us a cause for wonder that God could and did use a leader like Samson even against so brutal and noncivilized a people as the Philistines. But the best of us have weak spots at times as is seen in the case of Simon Peter. Even Paul called himself the " chief of sinners." We are all sinners saved by grace. Only, let us not deceive ourselves by thinking that the fact that God does use sinful men in his service absolves us from the obligation to be holy unto the Lord. God used Samson in spite of his sins, not because of them. And his sins became his undoing in the end.

2. A Man of Passion and Power.

He was clearly a man of vigorous health and vitality, of energy and physical prowess. But, besides this, " the Spirit of the Lord came mightily upon him " (Judges 14: 6) at times so that he was then endowed with more than human strength. This is the wonder of the man, how God used him thus single-handed to throw off the oppression of the Philistines from time to time. The youth David slew Goliath, also a leader of the Philistines, with a stone from his sling, flung with unerring skill. But the feats of Samson are of a different sort and seem more like the prowess of brute force. A young lion came across his path and with nothing in his hand Samson rent him as he would a kid. Later he ate the honey that a swarm of bees made in the carcass of the lion and made a riddle: " Out of the eater came forth food, And out of the strong came forth sweetness." When his Philistine wife betrayed the secret of the riddle, the Philistines solved it for him. He said roughly: " If ye had not plowed with my heifer, Ye had not found out my riddle." Then " the Spirit of the Lord came mightily upon him, and he went down to Ashkelon, and smote thirty men of them, and gave the changes of raiment unto them that declared the riddle." Fierce vengeance it would seem to us. When his wife was taken from him he took 300 foxes, bound their tails together, set them on fire, and turned them loose in the ripe grain of the Philistines, a mad freak of revenge. After the Philistines burned his wife and father-in-law, " he smote them hip and thigh with a great slaughter." His justification to the men of Judah for his conduct to the Philistines was a sort of heathen version of the Golden Rule: " As they did unto me, so have I done unto them." They had said it first to the men of Judah. When bound by the men of Judah to be turned over to the Philistines, " the Spirit of the Lord came mightily upon him " (15: 14) and he snapped the two new ropes like flax touched by fire and with a fresh jawbone of an ass smote a thousand Philistines as they burst upon him at Lehi. At Gaza he escaped from the Philistines by plucking up the posts of the gate, bar and all, and carrying them to the top of the mountain before Hebron (16: 3). Samson was strong when the power of God came upon him. He knew that he was strong and defied his enemies. It is so easy to assume one's strength as a matter of course, to make a display of it for selfish purposes. There is peril in power, even in the power of the Lord.

3. Samson Presumed on His Strength.

He knew his unusual power and that was his danger. He knew the vow under which he laboured and did his exploits, of which his long hair was the symbol. His weakness was women, and Delilah, another woman of Philistia, enticed him to betray the secret of his great strength as his former wife enticed him to reveal the secret of his riddle. See the mighty man as his head lies in Delilah's lap and she plays with his hair in her efforts to learn the secret of his power in order to rid him of it. She begins to tempt him and whisper in his ear: " Tell me, I pray thee, wherein thy great strength lieth, and wherewith thou mightest be bound to afflict thee." He does not mean to tell her, for he knows it will be his downfall, but he dallies with the temptation as a child with a soap bubble. He will just try her patience a bit. " If they bind me with seven green withes that were never dried, then shall I become weak, and be as another man." She had Philistines lying in wait in the inner chamber. So she cried: " The Philistines are upon thee, Samson." But he broke the withes like a string of tow touching the fire. He was still secure and enjoyed deceiving Delilah. But she persevered as the tempter always does. " Thou hast mocked me, and told me lies. Now tell me, I pray thee, wherewith thou mightest be bound." This time he said: " If they only bind me with new ropes wherewith no work hath been done, then shall I become weak and be as another man." So she called again: " The Philistines are upon thee, Samson." He broke the ropes like a thread.

Once more Delilah attacks him with her wiles: " Hitherto thou hast mocked me, and told me lies: tell me wherewith thou mightest be bound? " Lightly again he mocked her with a lie: "If thou weavest the seven locks of my head with the web." He was coming close to telling the truth this time, but not quite. "She fastened it with the pin and said unto him, the Philistines are upon thee, Samson." He had been asleep, but he "plucked away the pin of the beam, and the web." He still had his strength. Three times he had toyed with temptation and was still the same strong man. But the end is not yet. Delilah is not through with Samson. She is like a cat toying and purring with a bird. "Let him that thinketh he standeth take heed lest he fall." Peter boasted to Jesus that he would die before denying him and yet denied him before dawn.

4. *Samson Shorn of His Strength.*

Delilah would not give up. Women rarely give up. She had lured Samson on thus far. She will try once more. "How canst thou say, I love thee, when thy heart is not with me? Thou hast mocked me these three times, and hast not told me wherein thy great strength lieth." Samson should have been warned by the persistence of Delilah, by the fact that she was a Philistine, by his previous experience about the betrayal of the secret of his riddle, by the sacredness of his vow as a Nazirite, by the use that God had for his strength against the Philistines to save Israel. But, as always when a strong man yields to temptation and falls, all the good reasons that should hold one back from evil vanish into thin air before the lure that draws one over the abyss. "And it came to pass, when she pressed him daily with her words, and urged him, that his soul was vexed unto death." She had become a habit with him, like the liquor or the morphine habit. She came upon him with relentless energy and renewed force like the demon that came back with seven other spirits worse than himself so that the last end of that man was worse than the first. This is the way of evil habits as every drunkard knows. In an untoward moment, when he was weary and unwary, " he told her all his heart," told her to get rid of her vexatious nagging and in so doing broke faith with the God whose Spirit gave him his power. " There hath not come a razor upon my head: for I have been a Nazirite unto God from my mother's womb: if I be shaven, then my strength will go from me, and I shall become weak, and be like any other man " (16: 17). Delilah now saw that he had indeed told her all his heart. She had carried her point at last and had won over this weak strong man and was sure of his ruin. Little she cared for his love now that she knew his secret. So " she made him sleep upon her knees: and she called for a man, and shaved off the seven locks of his head; and she began to afflict him, and his strength went from him." Once more she cried in triumphant glee: " The Philistines are upon thee, Samson." He awoke out of his sleep, unconscious of what had been done to him, but knowing full well that he had betrayed his vow to the Lord. " I will go out as at other times, and shake myself free." He was like the drunkard who had always gotten over his previous sprees and debauches. But his strength was gone. At first, " he knew not that the Lord was departed from him." His strength was not in his hair, but from God. The hair was simply the sign of his vow under which he lived. He had broken his vow to the Lord and the Spirit of God left him alone in his own natural weakness. He was helpless before the Philistines now. They took him, put out his eyes, brought him down to Gaza, bound him with fetters of brass, and made him grind the mill like an ox, this once mighty man of valour.

5. *The Tragedy of His Downfall and Death.*

It was all due to Delilah, no doubt Samson now argued in his blindness. Yes and no. He could have resisted Delilah once. That was at the start. It is the first drink that is the beginning of the drunkard's career. It is the first crime that begins the criminal life. Modern physiological psychologists emphasize the power of habit, even of evil thoughts that leave a mark upon the brain and nerve tissues and invite a return of thought and deed. Elisha was sitting in his house and the messenger of the king was heard coming. " Look, shut the door and hold him fast at the door. Is not the sound of his master's feet behind him? " That is the only safe way to treat the first messenger of the tempter. Satan himself is not far in the rear. There is an old Latin proverb that " one sin treads on the heels of another." Sin goes in packs like wolves. One yell is the sign of others close by. The Cherokee Indians have a legend that on one of the islands in the French Broad River there once lived a siren that sang so sweetly that hunters would listen and be lured to destruction. It is the old story of Ulysses again. It is hard to get the ear of those who rush on heedlessly over the rapids, confident that they are safe in spite of the Niagara before them. " Get thee behind me, Satan," Jesus said. This is the only safe way in temptation. God would not go with Samson when he had broken his vow of consecration as a Nazirite. God could no longer use him. That solemn lesson awaits some of God's servants who fall into sin. They are shorn of power when they go forth without God to do the Lord's work. The Spirit of the Lord is not with us then. We wonder sometimes if modern Christians are not powerless because of the absence of God's Spirit who finds no pleasure in our lives of ease and of sin.

Samson's loss of strength came soon after his greatest exploits. Pride goes before a fall. Victory can demoralize an army as readily as defeat. The tempter may come as a wolf in sheep's clothing. " Let nothing pass," Napoleon commanded the pickets one night. A dog came and the picket hesitated. He shot him and it was a man in a dog's skin, come to play the spy within the lines. "Pray that ye enter not into temptation," Jesus urged in Gethsemane. He knew the power of the tempter as no one else did.

Only once did God give back strength to Samson. He was in the temple of Dagon, the god of the Philistines, where they were making sport with Samson who so often had triumphed over them. Samson asked the lad who was leading him to place him between the two pillars. Then he prayed God for power again. "O Lord Jehovah, remember me, I pray thee, and strengthen me, I pray thee, only this once, O God, that I may be at once avenged of the Philistines for my two eyes" (16: 28). He pleaded again: "Let me die with the Philistines." God heard this despairing cry, and the house fell upon the lords of the Philistines, the crowds in the house, and upon Samson. Moreover, three thousand on the roof perished also. "So the dead that he slew at his death were more than they that he slew in his life." A sad triumph was that.

Dr. James Stalker finds six classes of the tempted, three on the right, three on the left. On the left are those that are being tempted, those that are yielding to temptation, those that are leading others to temptation. On the right are those that are resisting temptation, those that have outgrown some temptations, those that are helping others to overcome temptation. Where do you come in, my friend, in this eternal battle? Satan left Jesus "for a season," until another opportunity. Like Delilah he keeps on coming back. "Get thee behind me, Satan."

XVII

PAUL'S PLANS FOR RAISING MONEY

"See that ye abound in this grace also."—2 CORINTHIANS 8: 7.

CHAPTERS eight and nine of Second Corinthians are the best handbook for raising money for church purposes ever written by any one. Once before Barnabas and Paul took a collection for the poor saints in Jerusalem from the Gentile church in Antioch. It had a wholesome effect on the Jewish Christians as proof that these Gentiles in Antioch were really Christians. Indeed they were first called Christians in Antioch. The Judaizers, the extreme party in the Jerusalem church, insisted that Gentile Christians should become Jews also. Even after the decision in Paul's favour at the Jerusalem Conference, they caused suspicion and misrepresentation about Paul's motives and purposes and opposed his whole missionary work. Paul of his own accord, because of the great need in Jerusalem and to conciliate other Jewish brethren who were misled by the Judaizers, raised a great collection from the Gentile Christians in four Roman provinces (Asia, Galatia, Macedonia, Achaia, the Roman name for Greece) where he had laboured. He gives here in 2 Corinthians 8 and 9 the reasons why the Corinthians should participate in this offering at this time. Here is always the problem for pastors of churches and denominational representatives, how to get this particular church at this exact time to share in this collection for this particular object. There are so many loopholes in time, place, purpose that it is increasingly hard to put the collection across, as every pastor knows. Paul handles the problem in superb fashion. He urges the collection:

160

1. *Because of the Liberality of the Macedonians.*   8. 1—5

Paul has no hesitation in appealing to church rivalry in the matter of giving. He disposes at once of the common excuse for not giving, that the church is poor, with no rich members, the times are hard. It is an amazing story that he tells at once of " the grace of God " (his name all through the argument for the collection) among the churches in Macedonia. The points pile up in overwhelming style. The Macedonian churches had given in the midst of " much proof of affliction " for they had suffered persecution. They gave out of " their deep poverty," poverty that reached down deep like a well, days of depression. Philippi was a poor city as compared with Corinth (a great commercial city). Even Thessalonica was not equal in wealth to Corinth. But, in spite of these two serious troubles, there was " abundance of their joy " that " overflowed unto the riches of their liberality." It was the joy that turned the poverty into riches of liberality. Objections and excuses were swept away by the flood of joy. Paul bears witness again that they gave " according to their power," as all should (tithers, at any rate, they were), " yea, and beyond their power." Paul clearly was not opposed to high-pressure collections now and then, especially in a case like this when people give " of their own accord " (voluntarily) and with a note of urgency demanding the privilege of sharing in the collection, " beseeching us with much entreaty in regard to this grace and the fellowship in the ministering to the saints." " The Macedonian Christians did not wait to be asked to give; they asked to be allowed the privilege of giving " (Bernard). It might be that Paul was at first unwilling to take so generous an offering from people who were so poor. But they had learned, as Jesus taught, that it is more blessed to give than to receive. But Paul had a still greater surprise. They went beyond his expectations, for we should say, " not as we had expected " (instead of " hoped "). " First they gave their own selves to the Lord, and to us through the will of God." First in importance, first of all, they consecrated themselves to the Lord in complete surrender and then put themselves at the command of Paul, from love and personal gratitude to him. This is the secret that many churches have never learned. They look on giving as a burden and object to having to raise money for causes outside of their own community. It is small wonder that covetousness and stinginess hamper the efforts of all denominations to raise money for missions and education. Self-interest and selfishness drown out the call for generosity. We make too often a distinction between the spiritual phases of the gospel and the grace of giving. Paul's whole point centers in the fact that giving is the grace of God, given by God, one that is itself a spiritual experience and is the result of the work of the Holy Spirit in our hearts. The regularly organized work is sometimes carried on in too mechanical a way and sometimes fails at this very point where some of the independent or " faith " missions succeed, for they press the spiritual aspect as their chief reliance.

2. Because They Should Pay What They Promised.

The churches in Achaia were the first to pledge a gift to this cause under the influence of Titus over a year ago. He went with Paul's approval, but " of his own accord." The promise to give was a fine thing. Paul is not objecting to that at all. Only they should pay what they promised. They were like F. Hopkinson Smith's *Col. Carter of Cartersville,* who readily gave his promises or note which he never paid, for he could not imagine how any one would wish anything better than a note with his name signed to it. I have known pastors of churches who repeatedly pledged their churches for certain sums, none of which was ever paid. They evidently cared more for the credit of liberality in the

convention assembled than for the duty of paying.
Credit falls when payment is not made. In some states
public subscriptions are usually discounted fifty per
cent. The charge is laid on Titus to go back to Corinth
and to finish what he began. The Corinthians were the
first to promise and the last to pay, if indeed they ever
did pay. No names from Achaia are given by Luke in
Acts 20: 4 when he names the messengers going with
Paul to carry the collection to Jerusalem. This reluctance to give on the part of the wealthy Corinthians
is sometimes encountered to-day. Paul presses the point
to the extent of saying that, if the Corinthians do not
pay up what they so readily pledged over a year ago,
he will be put to shame by them (9: 1–5). He had
boasted of their readiness to pledge and had thus stirred
the poor Macedonians to actual and surprising liberality.
He is coming soon to Corinth and may bring with him
some Macedonians. If they are still behind in Corinth,
Paul says that he will be ashamed of them even if they
are not ashamed of themselves. Some people have no
sense of shame about not paying church subscriptions.
It is a curious kind of psychology as if God does not
know or does not care. "Your zeal [in pledging
promptly] stirred up [stimulated] the more part [of the
Macedonians]." "It is superfluous for me to write to
you" (9: 1), but all the same he does it and with great
pungency and power, even if with small success in
Corinth. It is like trying to get blood out of a turnip
to get money out of some people. The church in Corinth
is a most gifted one. They had prophets, preachers, and
unknown tongues galore. "But as ye abound in everything, in faith and utterance and knowledge, and in all
earnestness, and in your love to us, see that ye abound
in this grace also." Paul's discussion of the many
spiritual gifts with which this remarkable church was
endowed is found in 1 Corinthians 12 to 14. How could
such a church fall behind in the pledges to this cause?

That puzzled Paul as it puzzles thousands of pastors to-day as they see the contributions to missions and education fall short. How could they resist Paul's plea? There had been serious disturbances in the life of the church in Corinth. At last these had been largely healed by the work of Titus. The great majority had finally swung round to the support of Paul, but the Judaizers still had a stubborn minority.

3. Because the Collection Is a Test of Their Love for Christ.

" As proving through the earnestness of others the sincerity also of your love." Giving is not the only test of one's love for Christ, but it is a real test. The word for " sincerity " here means genuineness as of money, or legitimacy as of birth. Actions speak louder than words, we say. Profession of love is good and necessary, but performance proves the quality of the profession. Chemists have acid tests for gold and silver. Doctors have tests for the blood, the heart, the lungs. Fool's gold looks like real gold, but you cannot depend on its face value. Money talks in religion as in business. Paul does not hesitate to present clearly and sharply this point. There is a type of piety that shies off when money is mentioned. It used to be considered bad form in some churches to have a collection taken in church during the worship for fear it might disturb the spiritual emotions of those in church. Even to-day we usually have the collection before the sermon to get it out of the way of the sermon. There is such a thing as a money test of the genuineness of one's profession of love for Christ. Let us face it squarely. Is our love worth a hundred cents on the dollar? Paul strikes at the very heart of stinginess and covetousness. He puts the sincerity of their love to the proof. In every relation of life love prompts to giving. And giving is a test of the sincerity of our words of love.

4. *Because of the Example of Jesus.*

"For ye know the grace of our Lord Jesus Christ, that, though he was rich, yet for your sakes he became poor, that ye through his poverty might become rich" (8: 9). No words could be more beautiful. The previous rich estate of Jesus Christ with the Father in heaven was voluntarily exchanged for that on earth where the Son of God did not have where to lay his head when he left the home in Nazareth. We have only to refer to Philippians 2: 6 to 11 to see the full commentary on this beautiful verse: "Who, existing in the form of God, counted not the being on an equality with God a thing to be grasped, but emptied himself, taking the form of a servant, being made in the likeness of men." Clearly Paul had no doubt about Christ's preexistence and about the incarnation, any more than Jesus himself had (John 17: 5). It is not the picture of one who "became God" that we have here, but of the Son of God "become man." "The ineffable surrender was made for you" (Plummer). It was not mere hardship and penury that Paul here has in mind, but the humble estate of his humanity in contrast with the supreme glory with his Father. "He became poor when he entered the world, with a definite purpose to enrich his disciples, not in earthly goods, but in the same riches He Himself originally possessed in the heavenly world" (Briggs). Paul gives no command concerning the example of Christ as an incentive to liberality. If the example of Christ will not spur and incite them to liberality, then nothing will do so. We can be too sensitive about the place of money in kingdom work. Where does God come in in our financial budget? The government levies the income tax. Christ appeals to our love for him. If we shut our eyes and dodge the issue, we are robbing God. "Thanks be to God for his unspeakable gift." That supreme gift of love calls for a response on our part.

5. *Because of the Principle of Proportionate Giving.*

2 Co 8 12

" For if the readiness is there, it is acceptable, according as a man hath, not according as he hath not." That is the principle of proportionate giving. One who has nothing is not expected to give. I once knew a church that gave a small stipend to each member who contributed nothing to the church funds with the idea that, unless in real want, one will give. But Paul does insist that we give up to our own ability, not down to our stingy needs. He lays down no definite amount for any individual, but leaves it to his conscience according to the actual facts. The income tax will help any one to find out what his real income is. Paul does not name the tithe of the Old Testament. But surely grace should do as well as law. It ought to do better. The tithe for the Christian should be the minimum, not the maximum. The very rich should give very much more than a tenth as the income tax rises rapidly in such cases. But if church members to-day actually gave a tithe of their income, the denominational boards and schools and churches would overflow with money for the Lord's cause. Paul's point is that equality in liberality does not mean the same amount for each one. He does not desire that some shall be oppressed while others go free. They should bear in mind also that riches take wings and often fly away, sometimes overnight, as millions know to their sorrow. Your abundance at the present time can be a supply for the poor saints in Jerusalem. But the tables may be turned some day when their abundance will be a supply for your want. These are words of wisdom for the proud and self-satisfied man without a liberal heart.

6. *Because the Money Will Be Handled Honestly.*

2 Co 8. 20-1

Titus was Paul's agent in the collection in Corinth. But the churches concerned had appointed another brother (Luke, Erastus, or some one else) to act as

their representative in the matter. Paul took this wise
precaution lest " any man should blame us in the matter
of this bounty which is ministered by us: for we take
thought for things honourable, not only in the sight of
the Lord, but also in the sight of man." Handlers of
religious funds are answerable to men as well as to God.
Careless keeping of books is inexcusable. Accurate
bookkeeping is right and wise. Any competent auditor
should be able to give a clear endorsement of all accounts. One of the lamentable facts of recent financial
troubles is the embezzlement of funds by church
treasurers. Distrust is thus caused on every hand. Paul
sent also another brother who was added to the two
already named (8: 22). The names of still others occur
in Acts 20: 4. These " messengers (*apostles,* literally)
of the churches " deserved a welcome and open endorsement " in the face of the churches," a thing that some
pastors avoid in the case of agents for denominational
causes. Besides sending agents Paul wrote letters and
made appeals in person. He was not ashamed to be a
collector of money for the Lord's work.

7. *Because of the Law of Sowing and Reaping.*

" He that sows sparingly will reap also sparingly; and
he that sows bountifully will reap also bountifully."
Every farmer knows this fact. It is axiomatic. There
is some risk in sowing, to be sure, but no sowing, no
harvest. Giving, therefore, should be a matter of principle and method, not done sporadically in a haphazard
way, not grudgingly, or of necessity as if one's eye-
teeth were being pulled out, but with a glad heart,
rejoicing at the opportunity and privilege. " For God
loves a cheerful giver," literally " a hilarious giver," one
who is having the time of his life in using some of his
substance for the Lord's work. There is joy in giving
at Christmas, as we all know. There was joy in Macedonia over giving. There should be joy in our hearts

2 Cor. 9.⁶

when we give. " God is able to make all grace abound unto you."

8.   *Because of the Gratitude Caused by It.*

The wants of the saints in Jerusalem will be filled up and satisfied. Their hearts will be stirred to fresh gratitude for God's mercies and for the dispensers of this grace to them. It is more blessed to give than to receive when you see the gladness of heart created by the giving. " They glorify God for the obedience of your confession unto the gospel of Christ, and for the liberality of your contribution unto them and unto all." They will, besides, pray for you, says Paul, and " long after you by reason of the exceeding grace of God in you." That experience will be a comfort and joy to the Corinthians if they win it by doing their part. Then all those who give and those who receive will say: " Thanks be to God for his unspeakable gift." Some will see the reflection of this grace in you. Giving is a grace from God and is like God. " For God so loved the world, that he gave his only begotten son, that whosoever believeth on him should not perish, but have eternal life."

XVIII

FIRST THINGS FIRST

"But seek ye first his kingdom, and his righteousness; and all these things shall be added unto you."—MATTHEW 6: 33.

IT is often difficult to see what is really first in importance in the duties of life. Sometimes they seem to come into sharp conflict. We are drawn this way and that, not simply by temptation to evil, but by the appeals of the good. The good is sometimes the enemy of the best. We have limitations of knowledge, of strength, of purpose. Dr. James Moffatt has a suggestive little book on *The Second Things of Life.* Sometimes they seem to take first place for the time being. Jesus constantly pressed upon men the duty of doing first things first. This problem constantly challenges us all both young and old.

1. *The Primacy of Christ Himself.*

Over and over again Jesus said: "Follow me." He said it to Matthew at the place of toll by the roadside. Jesus called himself the Light of the World, the Way to the Father, the Truth about the Father, the Life of men, the Judge of men, the Son of God, the Son of man, the Redeemer and Saviour from sin. Jesus accepted worship from Thomas as Lord and God. Paul places Jesus Christ at the head of the universe as Creator and Lord, as Head of the Church General, as very God manifested to men. There is no second place for Christ in the New Testament. He is first in nature and grace. The effort to-day to rank Jesus with Confucius, Buddha, Mahomet, and Zoroaster is in utter conflict with the claims of Christ himself and the teaching of the New Testament. Christianity is not just one of the religions of the world. It is the religion for the whole world, for " in none other is there salvation; for neither is there any other name under heaven, that is given among men, wherein we must be saved " (Acts 4: 12). " He is before all things, and in him all things consist. And he is the head of the body, the church: who is the beginning, the firstborn from the dead; that in all things he might have the preëminence " (Col. 1: 17f.), literally " that in all things he might himself become first." There is here almost a laboured effort to express the supremacy of Christ in nature and grace. There is no room beside Christ for any earthly teacher. He stands alone. The chief errors in early Christian teaching came from the Gnostics by " not holding fast the Head " (Col. 2: 19). So to-day Christianity is challenged by the new Unitarianism which seeks to present Christ as merely man's approach to God, not God's approach to man. The peril is real and great, but modern Christians know by blessed experience that Jesus is Lord and Saviour from sin. They will not disown Jesus Christ and go after strange gods. They will be true to Christ at home and keep on proclaiming him in pagan lands as the only hope of mankind in spite of superficial condemnation of the work of missions by men no longer true to Jesus Christ as the only Saviour from sin. Christ is first or nothing. He is the Revealer of God because he came forth from the bosom of the Father. He is the mystery of God in whom are all the treasures of wisdom and knowledge hidden.

2. Hence Christ's Kingdom Comes First.

If we sanctify Christ as Lord in our hearts, we will seek first God's kingdom and righteousness. The kingdom of God is Christ's kingdom. " My kingdom is not of this world," said Jesus to Pilate, but it stands above

and before all the kingdoms of earth. The problem
here is that the world of sense presses itself so constantly upon us that we allow the unseen to fade away
because of the seen. The pressure of the moment dims
the reality of the eternal.

(a)   A business life asserts its claims above the king-
        dom of God.

Church members are constantly prone to excuse themselves from the work of the kingdom because of the
claims of business. The club or the secret order is
allowed to come before the prayer-meeting. Golf takes
the place of church attendance. The automobile may
carry one away from church instead of to church. The
mad rush for money dulls the spiritual life till one is
unresponsive to the call of the church bell. " For what
shall a man be profited, if he shall gain the whole world,
and forfeit his life? Or what shall a man give in exchange for his life? " (Matt. 16: 26).

(b)   The family may come between one and the king-
        dom.

When Jesus challenged a certain man with his call,
" Follow me," the man agreed, but said: " Lord, suffer
me first to go and bury my father " (Luke 9: 59). That
was a pious filial duty which demanded attention. But
the man's father was still alive. What he meant, according to common Oriental usage, was a plea to remain
with his father till he should die and then after the
burial he would " follow " Jesus. This explains the
answer of Jesus: " Follow me; and leave the dead to
bury their own dead " (Matt. 8: 22), with the added
words in Luke (9: 60): " But go thou and publish abroad
the kingdom of God." The spiritually dead can bury
your father if need be, but following Christ is more
important than such a reverent service. Jesus clearly
means to put service to him before family obligations,

important as they are. Another man volunteered to follow Jesus: " I will follow thee, Lord; but first suffer me to bid farewell to them that are at my house " (Luke 9: 61). That seemed like a plausible excuse, but the Master replied: " No man, having put his hand to the plow and looking back, is fit for the kingdom of God." It is a proper enough thing to say good-bye to the home folks, but it does not rank with immediate service to Christ. The only way to plow a straight furrow is to look ahead and not back. Both of these men put home duties before following Jesus. One day Jesus startled the multitudes by saying: " If any man cometh unto me, and hateth not his own father, and mother, and wife, and children, and brethren, and sisters, yea, and his own life also, he cannot be my disciple " (Luke 14: 26). It is a matter of relativity. If any member of the family steps in between you and Christ, the choice is clear. Duty to Christ comes first. Fortunately in our own land, this test is not often made of our loyalty to Jesus. But it is made every day in China, India, Japan. Many a young man has to renounce home or Christ. One who does not take care of his family is worse than an infidel, Paul says, but there is a limit. Jesus says that he came to bring a sword, if necessary, to divide those in the same household, one from the other. Loyalty to Christ comes first, even before love for those at home.

(c) Christ comes before one's own life.

" If any man would come after me, let him deny himself, and take up his cross, and follow me " (Matt. 16: 24). He must be willing and able to say " no " to his selfish ambitions and desires if they conflict with following Christ. Jesus bore his own cross and he challenges us to do the same with our crosses when they come. We are not to use them as excuses for not following him, but rather to pick them up and come on after him. Long life is not necessarily a blessing, certainly not in itself the greatest of earthly mercies. In order to conserve the interests of the kingdom it may be necessary for us to give up our earthly life for Christ's sake. In the immortal paradox of Jesus we have this: "For whosoever would save his life shall lose it; and whosoever shall lose his life for my sake and the gospel's shall save it" (Mark 8: 35). Service to Christ comes first, even before life itself, dear as that is. A light-hearted volunteer came to Jesus and said: "I will follow thee whithersoever thou goest" (Matt. 8: 19). He little understood what was involved in his offer. So Jesus replied: "The foxes have holes, and the birds of the heaven have nests, but the Son of man hath not where to lay his head." Jesus was at this time an exile from Galilee. He wanted the man to count the cost before he really decided to follow him. Without such definite counting the cost one "cannot be my disciple," Jesus says. "Whosoever doth not bear his own cross, and come after me, cannot be my disciple" (Luke 14: 27). The Master illustrated this profound saying by a man proposing to build a tower. He must "first sit down and count the cost, whether he hath wherewith to complete it." (The Bunker Hill monument was halted twice for lack of funds.) Otherwise, on his failure to finish it, men will mock him: "This man began to build, and was not able to finish." How many unfinished Christian lives lie in ruins about. They started off well in a burst of enthusiasm, but did not comprehend the cost of real service to Christ. The same point Jesus made with the story of a king who rashly went to war when he had only ten thousand men against twenty thousand. The losses in our church rolls are abnormally large. So many are quitters, slackers, deserters.

3. The Peril of Delay in Deciding for Christ.

Procrastination is the thief of time, the old adage runs, and it is only too true as many a lost soul knows. It is probable that more people fail to enter the kingdom of God for this reason than for any other. They do not seek first the kingdom of God, either in rank or in time. They acknowledge the claims in the abstract and really mean to accept Jesus as Lord and Saviour sometime, only this is not the convenient season. Minor matters crowd out a decision and postpone action till it is too late. By and by habit grips one as in a vise and one runs out his life in a groove of indifference to the claims of Christ. Locked in a shell of complacency it becomes hard for one to burst through and take an open stand. Once it would have been comparatively easy when the Spirit of God called earnestly and you almost yielded, but now it would take a small earthquake to wake you out of your stupor. When the worst comes to the worst, such an one clings to the hope of being after all a secret disciple of Christ. There were some rulers who " believed on him (Jesus) ; but because of the Pharisees they did not confess it, lest they should be put out of the synagogue; for they loved the glory of men more than the glory of God " (John 12: 42f.). Two of these timid disciples, Joseph of Arimathea and Nicodemus, took an open and bold stand for Christ when he was crucified and claimed the privilege of burying his body. How much better it would have been if they had openly avowed their love and their faith in him while he lived. Jesus demands confession of him as Saviour here and now: " Every one therefore who shall confess me before men, him will I also confess before my Father who is in heaven. But whosoever shall deny me before men, him will I also deny before my Father who is in heaven " (Matt. 10: 32f.). Jesus is the touchstone for every life in all the ages. He is set, as old Simeon saw, for the falling and rising of many, yes, of all. Some even idly imagine that they are on Christ's side. The problem of Pilate is the major question for every soul: " What shall I do with Jesus? " There is no way of evading a stand on this issue. "He that is not with me is against me."

One of the most pitiful of all of Christ's parables is that of the five foolish virgins who meant to be ready to greet the bridegroom when he came. They had neglected to procure oil for their lamps and slept as the bridegroom tarried in his coming. When all of a sudden his coming was announced, they tried frantically to borrow some oil from the five wise virgins who had oil in their lamps, but it was in vain. So they had to hurry off to buy some from the shops and when they at last returned, "the door was shut" (Matt. 25: 10). They cried aloud: "Lord, Lord, open to us," but in vain. The Lord answered: "Verily I say unto you, I know you not." The point of this parable plainly is that good intentions are not enough. Preparation must be made before it is too late and there is no hope after the door is shut. Those who cling to the hope of another chance after death, get no comfort from this parable. "Watch therefore, for ye know not the day nor the hour." After that it is too late. The lesson is so plain that he who runs may read. Put the first thing first and do it now.

The first thing that Andrew did after he found Jesus to be the Messiah was to go and tell his brother Simon. He did this "first" (*prōton*) before doing anything else: "This one first finds his own brother Simon and says to him: We have found the Messiah" (John 1: 41). Probably John also brought his brother James to Jesus. Certainly the greatest thing that Andrew ever did was bringing his brother Simon to Jesus. He put the first thing first. If this noble example set by Andrew had only been followed through the ages, the world would have been won to Christ in one generation. Now, instead of one winning one for Christ, it often takes a hundred or even a thousand to win one.

Moreover, in one's expenditure of money as well as in his use of time, one should put Christ and his kingdom first. It is certainly wrong to give to Christ's cause only what is left of one's money or time. That attitude of mind usually leaves nothing for the Master. Foreign missions, for instance, should be in one's personal budget, and in a place of honour. In the devotional life, also, the old rule of reading a chapter in the Bible at bed-time is nothing like so good as the new stress on an early hour for the quiet time or the morning watch.

In our text please observe that the kingdom of God precedes righteousness and alone makes it possible. That is, the new heart precedes the new life. The reward here promised may be illustrated by Paul's experience, " poor, yet making many rich; as having nothing, and yet possessing all things " (2 Cor. 6: 10).

So the command of Jesus comes to each of us to keep on seeking first the kingdom or rule of God in our own hearts as righteousness and in the hearts of others for righteousness. When this comes to pass with all, no one will need to say, " Know the Lord," for all will love him and look and long for his appearing. Peace will be in the hearts of men and swords will indeed be turned into plowshares. Put Christ first in your life. He is the Alpha and the Omega, the Beginning and the End.

XIX

THE PRACTICE OF THE WORD OF GOD

"But be ye doers of the Word, and not hearers only, deluding your own selves."—JAMES 1: 22.

MY friend and beloved physician for many years, Dr. J. B. Marvin, used to be fond of saying that preachers preach while physicians practise. He meant in his witty way to say that some preachers only preach for others, and do not practise their sermons on themselves. Unfortunately this jibe is sometimes true. It can be retorted likewise some physicians, " quacks " for instance, have more professional pretence than performance with their patients. Certainly the highest type of both preacher and physician is the one who combines profession and practice. James here has in mind all believers in Christ and not just ministers of the word. And by " the word " he means the message of God whether written or oral or by clear divine guidance, just so it is God's message. We are all familiar with Brother Lawrence's famous book, *The Practice of the Presence of God*. James is pressing on us all the practice of God's word.

1. *Being Swift to Listen to It.*

" But let every man be swift to hear." James has in mind the preaching of the word of God and the occasional dulness of the hearers. Surely some sermons are soporific enough to put people to sleep, but James urges the eager attitude of the hearer, who should be " swift to hear." In Sirach (5: 11) we have the phrase " swift in thy hearing " and in *Pirke Aboth* (5: 18) we have

" quick to hear and slow to forget." It is likely that
the phrase was a kind of proverb, for the Greek
moralists urged a quick and attentive ear. Homer sang
of " winged words " and in Hebrews 5: 11 the writer
laments that the readers have " become dull of hearing "
(having no push in their ears). It is common to see a
horse prick up his ears to hear. The Indians have keen
and sensitive hearing that can distinguish the softest
footfall or stirring of a leaf. Dr. John A. Broadus had
a lecture on " The Art of Listening." It is one that
some people never learn. Jesus often asked people to
listen to what he was saying. " He that hath ears to
hear let him hear." That is what ears are for. A young
man once went to sleep while Paul preached yet longer
and longer and fell out of the third story window and
Paul restored him to life. There is more danger in
going to sleep on preachers now in case of accident.
The Greek idiom for paying attention is to hold the
mind steadily on a subject and that is often a hard thing
to do without a strain upon the mind.

But James adds " slow to speak." He means, slow
to begin speaking, not dulness after one does begin.
Zeno used to quote Pindar's observation that we have
two ears and one mouth and should therefore listen more
than we talk. We still have the proverb that speech is
silvern and silence golden, but most of us practice the
silver, not the gold, standard in speech. The rabbis had
a saying (*Qoheleth Rabba 5:5*): " Speech for a shekel,
silence for two; it is like a precious stone." Will Carle-
ton touches us all when he says:

" *Boys flying kites haul in their white-winged birds;*
You can't do that way when you're flying words.
Thoughts unexpressed may sometimes fall back dead;
But God himself can't kill them once they're said."

Who would not long to call back the unkind word,

especially when that one who heard it is dead? And then James adds another clause, " slow to anger." There are many sayings in the Jewish Wisdom literature about the connection between " control of speech and restraint of anger " (Ropes). One of the best is in Proverbs 15: 1: " A soft answer turneth away wrath; but a grievous word stirreth up anger." And one just as good occurs in Proverbs 16: 32: " He that is slow to anger is better than the mighty; and he that ruleth his spirit than he that taketh a city." Clearly James means to say that if one is slow to speak, his anger will cool off. It is like putting fresh coals on the fire to answer back in anger. There is such a thing as righteous indignation, but one is not promoting God's righteousness (a Pauline phrase) by bursting out in angry retorts over personal insults. The problem is always how to be angry and sin not, as Paul urged. Feuds and duels and murders thrive in the state of prolonged anger with violent words. There is a connection between anger and insanity as shown in the two uses of our words mad and madness and in the plea of temporary insanity as a defence of murder. Listen to Proverbs again (29: 20): " Seest thou a man that is hasty in his words? There is more hope of a fool than of him." And once more (17: 28): " Even a fool, when he holdeth his peace, is counted wise; when he shutteth his lips, he is esteemed as prudent." That is one way to be wise, and to gain a reputation for wisdom, by keeping our mouths shut. The owl is a case in point in contrast with the chatter of the parrot. But silence when angry is a price for wisdom too high for many people.

2. *The Rooted Word in Us.*

This is the picture of the mind and heart as the soil, the metaphor in Christ's wonderful parable of the sower. Some seed falls by the wayside and is quickly picked up by the birds, some on stony ground and sprouts quickly and withers as quickly, some on thorny ground and is soon choked by the thorns and briars (the cares of the world and the deceitfulness of riches), some on good ground and actually bears fruit. The first step is to listen to God's word. The next is to let it germinate and grow. The phrase here is "the implanted word." That means that the Word of God has taken root in God's garden (the soul of man). James pleads that we give the precious plant a chance to grow: "Wherefore putting away all filthiness and overflowing of wickedness, receive with meekness the implanted word, which is able to save your souls." Weed out of the garden all the noxious weeds that spring up so easily, such as pride and stubbornness. It is not enough to have good seed and good soil. There must be sunshine and rain and proper cultivation to keep down the weeds. Perhaps pastors and parents and all Christians fail often here when they do not watch carefully enough the nurture of young Christians. The first years of all life are always the most important and difficult. They largely determine destiny.

3. *Bearing Fruit in Our Lives.*

"Keep on becoming," as you have started out to be, "doers of the word, and not listeners only," important as that is. Some people will not listen when God speaks and shut their ears and close their minds till their foolish hearts are blinded by the god of this world so that they cannot see the light of the glory of God in the face of Christ (2 Cor. 4: 6). It is a good thing to go to church to worship God and to hear the word of God proclaimed. But some avoid sermons as they do a plague. Some go once a day ("oncers"), while some do not go at all. But one may hear many sermons and by continued failure to respond become gospel-hardened and be worse off than before. The gospel is a savour of life unto life or of death unto death. Every sermon leaves one better or worse. But even good listening comes to naught if it does not find expression in the life. The mere tickling of the emotional nature may be a positive harm if not expressed in action. Our word "poet" is the very word used here by James for "doer." Emerson stressed the importance of the thinker and the sayer being also the doer. Some listen and forget, hear and do not heed, idle hearers. Paul (Rom. 2: 13) makes a contrast between "hearers of the law" and "doers of the law." James does here. But Jesus did it before them in the closing words of the Sermon on the Mount when he likens the man who hears his words and does them to a man who builds his house on the rock, and the man who hears and does not to one who builds his house on the sand (Matt. 7: 24–27). Such men delude themselves but no one else. James draws a striking picture of such an one who is like a man giving a hasty glance at his face in the glass and off he is gone and at once forgot what he looked like in the glass. He means man as distinct from woman. Such careless hearers are the soil by the wayside, where the birds picked up the seed as soon as it fell there. The real student of God's word pores over it until he enters into the meaning of this "perfect law of freedom," having thus become "not a hearer marked by forgetfulness, but a doer of deeds." This is the wise hearer who puts into practice what he has heard and reproduces in action the word of God. Actions speak louder than words, we say. This is the truly wise man whose deeds confirm his words. Such a man finds abiding happiness in doing the will of God. This beatitude belongs to the doer, not to the mere idle listener.

4. Complacent Religiosity Not Enough.

Here is another peril in the path of the truly pious and devout. Even the man who practises the Word of God is exposed to danger, that of professional piety or merely external ceremonial observances. The Pharisees were sharply condemned by Jesus for this very thing in performing righteous deeds such as alms, prayer, fasting, " to be seen of men " (Matt. 6: 1, 2, 5, 16). Philo holds that liberal gifts alone will not entitle one to " be reckoned with the pious; for he has also erred from the path of piety, accounting worship a substitute for sanctity." He uses the very same root for " worship " (*thrēskeia*) that James has for " religious " (*thrēskos*, an adjective found nowhere else). The idea is the outward observance of religious rites, things that are good in themselves (like attendance on public worship and beneficence), but do not take the place of inward piety. This Pharisaic touch appears as a constant danger in Christian worship, to consider observance of forms to be real worship of God. This is religion by rote, by rules, by rites, by letter without spirit. " If any man thinketh himself to be religious," as he ought to be, he must take pains to live up to his public profession. James singles out one item in ethics that is inconsistent with the public worship of God, the loose use of the tongue, " not bridling his own tongue." There is a reference to verse 19, " slow to speak." This is the earliest instance known of the word for " bridling " (*chalinagōgōn*), though it occurs later in Lucian. It is a bold and vivid picture of a man putting the bridle (*chalinos*) in his own mouth that he may be able to control his own tongue. James uses the same metaphor at more length in 3: 3f. and explains that, as with horses, so with us, the whole body is guided by the mouth. The man who does not put the bridle of self-control in his own mouth deceives himself, like the hearers only (verse 22) " deluding themselves." Professional pietists usually have a kind of conceit which increases with the constant repetition of their confessions and observances. Such a religious exercise with a loose tongue is a vain performance in the eyes of God and man. It lacks the note of reality. An unbridled tongue is proof of a heart

uncontrolled by the Holy Spirit. The tongue is an index
of the inner man with more certainty than external
observances of religion. It is not the only index by any
means, but it is a most common one. Hypocrisy is the
sin pictured here by James, that terrible sin of the
professedly "righteous" so mercilessly exposed by Jesus
in Matthew 6 and 23. There is a stock story of a deacon
with a grocery who asked the serving boy if he had put
the sand in the sugar and the pebbles in the coffee, and,
if so, to come on to morning prayers. That deacon's
"religious exercise" is the type so graphically condemned by James.

One can be complacent with his religious exercises
(religiosity) when the root of the matter is not in him.
He may be unkind to his family, unjust to his employees,
unfair and dishonest in his business dealings, and yet
be a regular attendant at church and even stay awake
during the sermon.

5. *Personal Purity Demanded.*

James adds an illustration (not a definition) of "pure
religion and undefiled before our God and Father." It
is God's eye that passes on our acts of religion and his
judgment is according to the realities in the case, not
the outward profession or pretence. The decision comes
from God and is therefore just. There are many instances in the papyri and the inscriptions of this word
"religious" for ritual and reverential worship. The
idea of James is to show an instance of such an act of
worship that is clean within and without. He mentions
visiting the orphans and the widows (and in this order),
a thing that any man with any religious impulses at all
may do. A man who refuses to help orphan children is
hard hearted indeed. But this is an obvious and easy
test for the professional pietist who plumes himself on
his ceremonial observances of worship. Place before
him a case of actual need, some orphan children who

need help, some widows in dire distress, and note his reaction to this appeal. It is impossible to overestimate the contribution of Christ to the cause of womanhood and of children. A new heart of pity and of helpfulness has come into the world. The parable of the Good Samaritan has changed the attitude of the world. Now every city has its community chest for those in need. There are orphanages, homes for aged women, hospitals that care for the poor.

But there is a deeper test yet that James applies, " to keep oneself unspotted from the world." This is still harder to do, particularly in a world so soiled with sin as is ours. Once a favourite soap was extensively advertised as the way to have " spotless town." The blood of Jesus Christ does cleanse us from all sin (1 John 1: 7), but it is our task also to keep the stain of sin away so far as we can. Jesus knows that we have to live and labour in a world of sin. He does not wish that we be removed as anchorites like monks and nuns out of the world. We are to live in the world and at the same time to be not of it (John 17: 14f.). Christ knows how severely one can be tempted and yet not sin. He is able therefore to help us when tempted (Heb. 2: 18). Many of us live in towns where soft coal is burned and the soot gathers on face, hands and clothes. We must keep them clean and keep on doing so. One morning a man asked his wife if the collar he held in his hand was clean enough to wear again. Without turning to see she said: " If it is doubtful, it is dirty." Needless to say, he did not put that collar on. He asked because it was doubtful. He concluded that it was dirty. That test comes to us every day about many things, about a book, a play in the movies, a problem of conduct. To which side shall we give the benefit of the doubt? If it is doubtful, it is dirty. Better run the risk of leaning toward restraint from evil than leaning toward the evil with the gambler's chance that it may not be so bad after all. The point in this rich paragraph in the Epistle of James is precisely the note of sincerity and reality, to be faithful to the truth of God in heart, in word, in deed, not spasmodically, but as a habit and to the end. It is not one emotional experience that James describes, but a high plateau of living, walking with God in Christ through all the journey of life.

A missionary in Africa once gave some converts the Sermon on the Mount to learn by heart. When they came back to recite it, he said: " Now you must try to put it in practice." They replied: " We had to do that in order to learn it. It is all so strange and new that we could not understand it except by trying to do it."

XX

LIBERTY AND LICENSE

"For ye, brethren, were called for freedom; only use not your freedom for an occasion to the flesh, but through love be servants one to another."—GALATIANS 5: 13.

PAUL is greatly stirred over the situation in Galatia. Judaizing teachers have come among them trying to get the Gentile Christians under the Mosaic ceremonial law as necessary to salvation. He has shown in his letter that the gospel of Christ is justification by faith, not by works of the law. It is all of grace, not by legalism. The true children of Abraham, the heirs of the promise, are those who believe in Christ as Lord and Saviour, whether Jew or Gentile. The legalists are like children of Hagar, the bondwoman. Christians are the spiritual children of Sarah, the free woman.

1. The Call for Freedom.

"For freedom did Christ set us free," Paul passionately exclaims (5: 1). Then he repeats it (5: 13): "For ye, brethren, were called for freedom." The dative case of the word for freedom (*eleutheriāi*) brings out clearly the purpose in Christ's call. It was not for a new bondage of ceremonialism that Christ set men free from the slavery of heathenism. Paul catches the idea of Jesus, whether he had ever heard the words preserved in John 8 or not: "Ye shall know the truth, and the truth shall make you free" (verse 32); "If therefore the Son shall make you free, ye shall be free indeed" (verse 36). Christ is the great Emancipator of the spirit of man from the bondage of sin. He alone is able to break the fetters which bind us fast as the slaves of sin (Rom. 6: 20). The only real freedom for the soul of man is in joyous service to Christ as Lord and Master. Men learn to love the yokes of habit and of sin. He paid the price for our ransom with his own life (Mark 10: 45) ; the very word for " ransom " (*lutron*) was common as the price of a slave. Christ set us free. So then, says Paul, stay free: " Stand fast therefore " in your freedom. " Stand firm, stand upright, do not bow your necks to the yoke of slavery " (Lightfoot). Martin Luther says: " Whosoever believeth in Christ, the Son of God, he hath this liberty." The forces of evil are always trying to imprison the spirit of man, but the caged bird will be set free. Paul's challenge here " has found an echo in many a heart since. The Lutheran Reformation was an answer to it; so was the Scottish Covenant. The spirit of Christian liberty is eternal. Jerusalem or Rome may strive to imprison it. They might as well seek to bind the winds of heaven. Its home is with God. Its seat is the throne of Christ. It lives by the breath of His Spirit. The earthly powers mock at it, and drive it into the wilderness. They do but assure their own ruin. It leaves the house of the oppressor desolate " (G. G. Findlay). The true Christian, like the eagle, can never be content with bondage, once he has breathed the free air of the mountains of God with Christ.

2. The Peril of Bondage.

Paul is instant with his warning: " Be not entangled again in a yoke of bondage." The verb (*enechō*) is often used of catching birds or beasts in a trap or snare or net. Elsewhere it is employed of being enmeshed in tribulations. We are sometimes caught unawares in trials. But the Galatians were now free in Christ from the slavery of paganism. They were blind and fools to be caught in the net of Jewish ritualistic legalism.

The Judaizers had even circulated false reports that
Paul himself now advocated circumcision for the Gentile
Christians (verse 11). There were no lengths to which
they would not go in order to enslave the Galatians to
the law. So Paul puts the matter pointedly to them:
"If ye receive circumcision, Christ will profit you
nothing" (verse 2), you Gentile Christians, he means.
That is true for the simple reason that one who is
circumcised is " debtor to do the whole law." Now Jews
have to believe in Christ in order to be saved. Circumcision did not save the Jew nor will it save the Gentile.
As a matter of fact, if Gentile Christians take on the
ceremonial law in order to be saved, " ye are severed
from Christ, ye who would be justified by the law; ye
are fallen away from grace " (verse 4). They thus will
renounce Christ as Saviour and look to the law for
salvation. They will exchange grace for law. " Legalism
and Paulinism, the true and the false gospel, stand front
to front, reduced to their basest form, and weighed each
in the balance of its practical result—*Christ or Circumcision:* which shall it be? " (Findlay). Paul says it
again that there may be no reason for misunderstand-
ing: " For in Christ Jesus neither circumcision availeth
anything, nor uncircumcision; but faith working through
love " (verse 6). It is not dead faith, like assent to a
bare creed, that Paul has in mind, but a live faith like
that expounded by James, a faith in Jesus Christ that
works and that does it through love.

The pity of it all is, says Paul, that " ye were running
well " (5: 7). They welcomed Paul as if he were an angel
of God when he first preached to them (4: 14f.) and
would have plucked out their eyes for him if necessary.
But now some unknown disturber has come and has
already won some of them away from Christ. " Who
did bewitch you? " Paul exclaims. Some spell-binder
destroyed the picture of Christ that Paul drew before
their very eyes. " Who hindered you that ye should

not obey the truth?" They were running a smooth and
winning race, but some one "cut in" (*enekopsen*) on
them and threw them off the track. That metaphor of
"cutting in" on one was common in military operations.
The enemy was always keen to cut in and break the
line or destroy the road or the bridge. Paul has used
the same word for Satan's hindering (cutting in on) his
plans for coming to the Thessalonians (1 Thess. 2: 18).
Some able exponent of Pharisaic ceremonialism had
been in Galatia and was "the disturber" who was
troubling the brotherhood, but he "shall bear his judgment, whosoever he be" (5: 10). Clearly Paul did not
know who the man was who was thus violating the
agreement reached at the Jerusalem Conference of freedom from the Mosaic law for the Gentile Christians.
Paul was determined that this "yoke of bondage"
should not be placed upon the necks of the Gentiles.
So he sounds a bugle note of liberty that echoes on
through the ages, until now. It will reverberate forever.
Ever and anon a preacher, a layman, or a sister becomes
a disturber in a church with a new kind of yoke and
tries to start a new fashion, a fresh bondage. But those
who have tasted the sweets of freedom in Christ will
turn a deaf ear to such heretics.

3. The Peril of License.

"Ye were called for freedom." There is no doubt
about that, freedom from the ceremonial law of bondage,
freedom also from the slavery of sin (Rom. 6: 15–23).
But freedom in Christ does not mean license. "Only,"
he says, "use not your freedom for an occasion to the
flesh." That charge was constantly made against Paul's
doctrine of justification by faith, salvation by grace
instead of works. Men said that he discounted even the
moral law because of God's surplus of grace. In the
letter to the Romans written about the same time as
this to the Galatians, he refutes this charge in detail

and proves that we ought to be holy because we are
under grace. He shows it by the figure of death (dead
to sin as symbolized by baptism) and new life in Christ,
by the figure of slavery (no longer slaves of sin, but
slaves of righteousness and of God), and by the figure
of marriage (married not to the law, but to Christ as
his bride). The flesh needs little excuse for indulgence
to its demands and Paul's glorious doctrine of grace was
made by some " an occasion " to let loose the flood-
gates of self-indulgence afresh. In the Corinthian
church precisely such sinful excesses of a sexual nature
did occur. Some of the Galatians were of a passionate
temperament that would increase Paul's uneasiness
about them. To-day under the plea of personal liberty
men and women are excusing their indulgence in drink,
in gambling, in sexual sins, in the use of dope. They
become victims of sinful habits and liberty has sunk
into license.

"But through love be servants one to another."
There are perils in liberty, even liberty in Christ, unless
it bears the restraint of love for Christ and for men.
"Where faith has this operation, liberty is safe; not
otherwise. Love's slaves are the true freemen" (Findlay). The royal law of James (2: 8) is quoted by Paul
here: "Thou shalt love thy neighbour as thyself."
This one word is the summary of the whole law, for it
is impossible without love to God as Jesus taught and
as is involved in his Golden Rule of life (Matt. 7: 12).
Paul puts the case sharply enough: "But if ye bite and
devour one another, take heed that ye be not consumed
one of another." This internal conflict in a church
between brethren will not lead to victory for either side,
but to the extinction of both (Lightfoot). Dr. E. Y.
Mullins was fond of telling of two Florida snakes that
seized each other by the tail and swallowed each other
so that no snake was left in the end. That is precisely
what Paul means here by failure to control oneself in

relation to others. Liberty is not anarchy, but freedom
controlled by love for the good of all. Liberty in Christ
means an orderly growth in righteous living and personal holiness and power for service. Some modern
psychologists have advocated the absence of all restraint
in the training of children who are allowed to develop
with complete license according to their own instincts
and whims. The specimens that I have seen have been
lamentable to behold. It is a fine way to develop de-
generates and criminals, not useful citizens in our world
of sin.

4. The War Between the Flesh and the Spirit.

It is a war and the forces of the spirit and the forces
of the flesh face each other in continual battle array as
the word translated " are contrary " means. The will
of each " lusteth " against the other. Paul in Romans
7 and 8 pictures this vivid and hopeless struggle before
Christ came to the rescue, but now with the aid of
the Holy Spirit there is hope of victory. So here there
must be the surrender of our wills to the spirit of Christ.
We have a new leader (the Holy Spirit) whose leadership is shown by the fruits in our lives (20 to 24). The
fruits (deeds) of the flesh are equally manifest (19–21).
" By their fruits, ye shall know them." Stalker has two
delightful little volumes of sermons on *The Seven
Deadly Sins* and *The Seven Cardinal Virtues*, carrying
out the lists of the ancient writers. Here more than
seven are given in each list. There are sensual sins,
sins of idolatry, sins of personal relations and disposition, sins of revelling and drunkenness, a horrible list
all too manifest in modern life. The list of virtues is
headed by love and includes joy, peace, longsuffering,
kindness, goodness, faith, meekness, and ends with self-
control. There is a similar list in Peter's picture of the
developing Christian (2 Pet. 1: 5–7). But these glories
and virtues do not come all at once. They blossom

gradually as the flowering time comes in spite of cold and rough weather. Paul adds a significant conclusion: "And they that are of Christ Jesus have crucified the flesh with the passions and the lusts thereof." It is only when we are crucified with Christ that we can say as Paul did: "And it is no longer I that live, but Christ liveth in me: and that life which I now live in the flesh I live in faith, which is in the Son of God, who loved me and gave himself up for me." Then we come to know that "faith is the victory that overcomes the world." But this victory over the world of flesh and sin is possible only through Jesus Christ our Lord. So then we thank God for liberty and do not desire license. We thank God that Jesus is our Master and that we are his slaves to do his every will. In that we find our joy and gladness.

Printed in the United States of America.

Date Due